Rhodri Jones is a barrister at St John's Chambers. He specialises in clinical negligence and inquests, acting for both claimants and defendants. Before retraining as a barrister Rhodri practiced as a medical doctor for 18 years, principally in A&E and general practice.

A Practical Guide to Material Contribution in Clinical Negligence

A Practical Guide to Material Contribution in Clinical Negligence

Dr Rhodri Jones

Barrister

MBChB MCEM MRCGP

Law Brief Publishing

Published 2023 by Law Brief Publishing, an imprint of Law Brief Publishing Ltd
30 The Parks
Minehead
Somerset
TA24 8BT

www.lawbriefpublishing.com

Paperback: 978-1-916698-13-0

To Flora, Willamina and Sylvester whose contributions are always material to me.

PREFACE

The application of the law of causation to medicine is intriguing. Not least because it represents an attempt to impose logic on matters where the underlying processes themselves are not fully understood. Many of the cases in which the application of material contribution has been successfully and unsuccessfully deployed were found on their facts.

The subject matter of this book does not naturally lend itself to a prescriptive practical approach. A practitioner faced with a case in which an injury or disease appears to have been materially contributed to by negligence needs to be equipped with a broad understanding of the key cases. The aim of this book therefore is to explore the reasoning behind the decisions of the courts (both in occupational disease and clinical negligence) and how that reasoning has been applied in recent cases. I hope that this book has succeeded in identifying the key concepts, themes and constructs that have emerged.

The rules in material contribution causation are not fixed. The application of material contribution to clinical negligence continues to develop. The recent High Court cases of *Thorley v Sandwell and West Birmingham NHS Trust [2021] EWHC 2604* and *Davies v Frimley Health NHS Foundation Trust [2021] EWHC 169* have attracted the attention of claimant and defendant commentators. It is likely that a suitable clinical negligence case will be taken to the Supreme Court to provide some clarity on the issue of whether the divisibility or indivisibility of a disease or injury is a determining factor in the application of material contribution.

I have not sought to catalogue all of the first instance decisions in which material contribution has been applied. I apologise for any mistakes. The law is stated as of 1 August 2023.

Rhodri Jones
August 2023

CONTENTS

INTRODUCTION

Material contribution is a concept in legal causation that was first applied by the courts in cases of occupational disease litigation. The concept has gradually extended its reach to cases of clinical negligence. It applies to circumstances where in determining the cause of a of a particular injury of disease both negligent and non-negligent agents are potentially implicated. The precise factual circumstances in which material contribution can be applied in clinical negligence remain undefined and thereby a source of uncertainty for practitioners.

The determination of causation in clinical negligence cases can be a complex exercise involving the consideration of medical and epidemiological evidence. Many of the cases where material contribution has been successfully applied to establishing causation have been found on their facts. The jurisprudence of material contribution is confusing and attempts to define the key legal principles have on occasion resulted in inconsistency. The courts have provided assistance by indicating what material contribution is not.

The importance of the law in creating certainty was emphasised by Lord Nicholls in the case of *Fairchild:*

> "*...To be acceptable the law must be coherent. It must be principled. The basis on which one case, or one type of case, is distinguished from another should be transparent and capable of identification. When a decision departs from principles normally applied, the basis for doing so must be rational and justifiable if the decision is to avoid the reproach that hard cases make bad law...*"[1].

1 *Fairchild v Glenhaven [2002] UKHL 22 [36]*

It is anticipated that suitable material contribution case will reach the Supreme Court to provide clarity on the range of its application. Perhaps it is naïve to consider that a common framework can be established which can apply to the complex and diverse range of situations that are likely to arise. As stated by Laws LJ in *Rahman:*

> *"The problem at the heart of this case rests in the law's attempts to contain the kaleidoscopic nature of the concept of causation within a decent and rational system for the compensation of innocent persons who suffer injury by reason of other people's wrongdoings. The common law has on the whole achieved just results, but the approach has been heavily pragmatic"* [2].

The aim of this book is to set out the key findings of the courts where they have considered the principles of material contribution and the circumstances in which it can be applied. To understand the evolution of material contribution in clinical negligence cases one must first consider its origins in cases concerned with occupation disease.

[2] *Rahman v Arearose Ltd v University College London NHS Trust 2001 QB 315 [31]*

CHAPTER ONE

FUNDAMENTALS OF MATERIAL CONTRIBUTION

The need to establish causation

Any analysis of material causation in clinical negligence causation must start with the traditional formulation of causation. In *Fairchild,* Lord Bingham set this out:

> "*In the generality of personal injury actions, it is of course true that the claimant is required to discharge the burden of showing that the breach of which he complains caused the damage for which he claims and to do so by showing that but for the breach he would not have suffered the damage*"[3]

Establishing causation is thereby essential in all cases where an individual having sustained loss is seeking damages from a potential tortfeasor. Where a claimant brings a claim in personal injury of any kind, the burden is upon them to prove it on the balance of probabilities. Establishing legal causation may in some circumstances be complicated, but its essence is based upon common sense. As stated by Lord Reid in the case of *McGhee*:

> "*it has often been said that the legal concept of causation is not based on logic or philosophy. It is based on the practical way in which the ordinary man's mind works in the everyday affairs of life*" [4]

---

3 *Fairchild v Glenhaven [2002] UKHL 22 [8]*

4 *McGhee v National Coal Board 1973 S.C. (H.L.) [37]*

In the same case Lord Salmon referred to his own judgment in the case of *Alphacell Ltd:*

> "*The nature of causation has been discussed by many eminent philosophers and also by a number of learned judges in the past. I consider, however, that what or who has caused a certain event to occur is essentially a practical question of fact which can best be answered by ordinary common sense rather than abstract metaphysical theory*"[5]

The traditional test for causation in personal injury is the 'but for' test: absent the tortious acts or omissions of a defendant, a claimant would not on the balance of probability have suffered the particular injury complained of. An often cited albeit extreme example of the 'but for' test in action is exemplified in the case of *Barnett*[6]. The claimant had consumed a quantity of arsenic and having presented himself to hospital, he was negligently discharged. He later died of arsenic poisoning. The court found that applying the traditional 'but for' principles of causation, absent the negligence he would on the balance of probabilities have died in any event.

Most cases in clinical negligence will succeed or fail on the application of traditional probabilistic causation principles. 'But for' causation most readily applies to cases where a singular act or omission has been identified by the Claimant as the cause of their injury. In this type of case, a single causative agent is in operation.

A claimant's primary injury will often be reasonably well defined. Issues may however arise where the Claimant has gone on to develop further injuries, for example a chronic pain condition or a psychiatric injury. In those circumstances, the claimant may seek to invoke principles such as

---

5 *Alphacell Ltd v Woodward [1972] AC 824 [847]*

6 *Barnett v Chelsea & Kensington Hospital Management Committee [1968] 2 WLR 422.*

the "*eggshell skull*". Similarly, defendants may seek to invoke principles of foreseeability and apportionment. The concept of material contribution does not need to be considered in the vast majority of personal injury cases.

The need for an alternative test in causation

The courts have on occasion raised the question of whether material contribution can in fact be viewed as freestanding legal principle in causation. HHJ Auerbach giving judgment in the case of *Davies* stated in relation to material contribution:

> "*while Bonnington Castings was viewed in Bailey as establishing a novel principle, later authorities of the Court of Appeal, House of Lords and Privy Council view it as having resulted in an anomalous outcome, for peculiar reasons, and not as standing for any novel legal principle, distinct from the general jurisprudence on co-contribution to divisible or indivisible harms. This conclusion appears to me to accord with deep principle, and with the prevailing view at the highest level, ever since Fairchild, that it stands alone as an exception to orthodox principles, in a tightly circumscribed type of case*"[7]

Assuming that it is a legal principle, material contribution in causation may be applicable when, having considered the facts of a particular case, the 'but for' test is insufficiently sophisticated to provide an answer. These types of cases often involve diseases and injuries where gaps exist in the scientific understanding of the relevant underlying physiological and pathological process. In this respect, material contribution may be characterised as a necessary means of dealing with causation in complex injury and disease processes.

In the industrial disease case *Fairchild*, the conundrum for the Court of Appeal was to decide on the balance of probabilities which fibre or fibres

[7] *Davies v Frimley Health NHS Foundation Trust [2021] EWHC 169 [209].*

of asbestos from different sources caused the claimant's injury. Lord Bingham described this issue as the "*Rock of uncertainty*"[8]. *Sienkiewicz* was another case in which asbestos was the causative agent. Lord Roger described the predicament of the courts when facing inherent medical uncertainty equipped with only standard causation principles:

> "*Faced with the problem that, in the present state of medical science, a claimant can never prove his case to the standard that the law usually requires, a legal system may react in a variety of ways. It may simply adhere to its usual stance and say that, since the claimant has not proved on the balance of probability that the defendant actually caused his disease, the claim must fail…*"[9]

Lord Phillips also highlighted how in certain circumstances applying the "*but for*" test can lead to inherent unfairness to both claimants and defendants:

> "*It is a basic principle of the law of tort that the claimant will only have a cause of action if he can prove, on balance of probabilities, that the defendant's tortious conduct caused the damage in respect of which compensation is claimed. He must show that, but for the defendant's tortious conduct he would not have suffered the damage. This broad test of balance of probabilities means that in some cases a defendant will be held liable for damage which he did not, in fact, cause. Equally there will be cases where the defendant escapes liability, notwithstanding that he has caused the damage, because the claimant is unable to discharge the burden of proving causation*"[10]

---

8 *Fairchild v Glenhaven [2002] UKHL 22* [7]

9 *Sienkiewicz v Grief (UK) Ltd [2011] UKSC 10 [140]*

10 Ibid [16]

Scientific understanding and uncertainty

Legal analysis of how a disease or injury manifests is inherently dependent upon an understanding of the underlying science. The courts are reliant in this respect on the evidence of experts. Their function is in assisting the court to explain how a particular causative agent interacts with an individual's physiology to cause disease. In medical terms an agent causative of a disease may be referred to a pathogen and the process by which a pathogens acts upon an individual described as its aetiology or pathophysiology. Litigation in clinical negligence is led by principles of medical science and thereby limited by scientific uncertainty. In this way, the analysis of causation naturally evolves in step with the scientific understanding of disease processes.

AB[11] was a case involving historic exposure to radiation. Smith LJ confirmed the court's reliance on expert analysis of the likely extent of exposure to the radiation and to provide scientific and epidemiological evidence of the likely effect in relation to the injuries complained of. The case of *Davies* involved an alleged delay in the treatment of meningitis. HHJ Auerbach, considered the importance to the court in making its determination of understanding the aetiology of the disease process "*It therefore helps at the start, to get one's general bearings by reflecting on what the experts, and the literature, tell me about the broad characteristics of this particular disease*"[12].

In case of *CNZ*[13] the task for the court was to consider the effect of delays at birth upon the injury to the claimant where the relationship between the causative agent and the brain was beyond scientific knowledge. In that case, the expert evidence assisted Ritchie J in finding for the claimant by applying standard causation principles. In obiter he acknowledged

---

11 *AB v Ministry of Defence [2010] EWCA Civ. 1317*

12 *Davies v Frimley Health NHS Foundation Trust [2021] EWHC 169 [123]*

13 *CNZ (Suing By Her Father and Litigation Friend MNZ) v Royal Bath Hospitals NHS Foundation Trust and Another [2023] EWHC 19 (KB)*

that whilst gaps in the understanding of science would make causation difficult to prove, this was no bar to the court making an assessment of causation by applying the principles developed in occupational disease to clinical negligence.

Ritchie J identified five "*tricky causation issues*"[14] that can arise in cases where there are gaps in the scientific understanding:

i. Multiple causative factors, one negligent and the others non negligent (naturally occurring / idiopathic / genetic / environmental etc.).

ii. One known causative factor, part of which was an innocently inflicted and part of which was caused by the breach.

iii. Multiple different defendants responsible for exposing the claimant to the same causative factor.

iv. Multiple known risk factors.

v. Multiple different outcomes which can occur from one known causal factor.

The approach of the court in matters where medical science cannot prove as a fact the causative potency of a particular was explored by Lord Phillips in Sienkiewicz:

> "*Most claims for death or personal injury result from accidents. In such cases the cause of death or personal injury will seldom be in issue. A body of knowledge which I shall call "medical science" will enable a witness, expert in that science, to describe the precise mechanism by which the accident brought about the death or injury. I shall describe this as the "biological cause" of death or injury. It is sometimes referred to by the more general*

Ibid [339]

> *description of the "cause in fact". In some cases, however, medical science will not yet have identified the precise mechanism by which an injury gives rise to a particular physical consequence. In such cases it may be possible to deduce that there was a causative link between the two by evidence of what usually happens. Epidemiological evidence that a particular injury or disease usually follows a particular type of bodily insult may enable a court to conclude in a particular case, on balance of probability, that the former was caused by the latter. "Post hoc ergo propter hoc". A finding of causation based on such evidence is sometimes described as "the cause in law"*[15].

Lord Phillips highlights here the potential for a distinction between medical and legal causation. The applicable standard of the latter being whether an agent more likely than not caused the injury or disease.

Causative agents

In most personal injury cases there is a single recognised causative agent, most often a physical accident, from which all identifiable loss flows. In clinical negligence and occupational disease litigation there may be multiple agents and multiple tortfeasors each playing a potential causative role to the injury. In the case of multiple agents these are often distinguishable as negligent and non-negligent in origin. The status of the agent refers to whether it was born of a breach of duty. In the case of *Bonnington Castings*[16] both negligent and non-negligent causative agents were operating simultaneously to cause the claimant's injury. In that case the claimant worked in a brick kiln where both "*guilty dust*" and "*innocent dust*" coexisted. *Bonnington Castings* is widely regarded as a touchstone for cases concerning material contribution.

15 *Sienkiewicz v Grief (UK) Ltd [2011] UKSC 10 [6]*

16 *Wardlaw v Bonnington Castings [1956] AC 613*

In occupational disease cases, as was the case in *Bonnington Castings*, the damage and loss was caused by a single identifiable agent: dust. The only distinction between the dust was its origin. The argument in *Bonnington Castings* was the extent to which, if any, the defendant should be liable for the damage caused by the so-called "guilty dust".

Many industrial disease cases where material contribution has been pleaded have a similar fact pattern. The role of the court in such circumstances is the determination and apporting of liability between multiple potential sources of the same causative agent. In clinical negligence cases there may be a range of different potential causative agents in operation which can make the determination of causation, and any apportionment more complicated.

<u>The test for material contribution in clinical negligence</u>

The courts have applied themselves to define the principles of material contribution. The clearest iteration of the circumstances in a clinical negligence case in which material contribution may be applicable is set out Waller LJ in *Bailey:*

> "*If the evidence demonstrates on a balance of probabilities that the injury would have occurred as a result of the non-tortious cause or causes in any event, the claimant will have failed to establish that the tortious cause contributed. Hotson exemplifies such a situation. If the evidence demonstrates that 'but for' the contribution of the tortious cause the injury would probably not have occurred, the claimant will (obviously) have discharged the burden. In a case where medical science cannot establish the probability that 'but for' an act of negligence the injury would not have happened but can establish that the contribution of the negligent cause was more than negligible, the 'but for' test is modified, and the claimant will succeed*"[17]

[17] Bailey v MOD [2009] 1 WLR 1052 [46]

In accordance with Waller J's basic statement of principle, the circumstances required to establish causation applying material contribution are:

i. The inability of medical science to demonstrate on the balance of probabilities that "but for" the negligence the injury would not have occurred.

ii. The ability to demonstrate that the contribution of the negligence to the injury was more than minimal.

The standard upon which the more than minimal contribution requires to be proved is the balance of probabilities. The reference to *Hotson*[18] is to the exclusion of cases where on the balance of probabilities the damage would likely have occurred in any event (i.e., where "but for" the negligence the damage would still have occurred). The burden is upon the Claimant to prove that the causative agent caused damage.

"More than minimal"

The accepted threshold for a negligent causative agent applying material contribution is something more than a minimal contribution to the injury. It is important to bear in mind that whilst the threshold is more than minimal, to qualify as a causative agent in the first place it must be proved to have a causative role on the balance of probabilities. Given that the causative role of an agent that has materially contributed to an injury is an inherent unknown, it is perhaps unsurprising that the courts have not provided any consensus as to what might constitute *de minimis.*

In *Bonnington Castings* Lord Keith referred to the accumulation of dust for which the defendant bore responsibility as "*In cumulo it must have been substantial, though it might remain small in proportion*"[19]. In the same

[18] Hotson v East Berkshire Area Health Authority [1987] 3WLR 232

[19] Wardlaw v Bonnington Castings [1956] AC 613 [626]

case, Lord Reid considered the extent to which a contribution would need to operate to be "material".

> "*What is a material contribution must be a question of degree. A contribution which comes within the exception de minimis non curat lex is not material, but I think that any contribution which does not fall within that exception must be material*" [20]

In the case of *Saunderson* (a group litigation for personal injuries following a fire) Jay J referred to the threshold whereby an injury may be actionable as "*Ultimately, in my judgment, this must be a question of fact and degree. A transient, trifling, self-limiting, reversible reaction to an irritant is not "actionable injury" for the purposes of the law of tort*" [21]

Lord Reid in *Bonnington Castings* uses the word "*substantially*" in looking at both the effect of the "*guilty*" dust and the "*innocent*" dust. However, he concluded "*In my opinion it is proved not only that the swing grinders may well have contributed but that they did in fact contribute a quota of silica dust which was not negligible to the pursuer's lungs and therefore did help to produce the disease*"[22]

Lord Hoffman in *Gregg*, whilst referring to *Wilsher*[23] considered that "*The defendant was only liable if the lack of oxygen caused or substantially contributed to the injury*" [24]. When considering what the necessary threshold was for a material contribution, Waller LJ in *Bailey* questioned whether the use of the word "*substantial*" implied a higher requisite causative potency than simple *de minimis:*

---

20 Wardlaw v Bonnington Castings [1956] AC 613 [621]

21 *Saunderson & others v Sonae Industria (UK) Ltd [2015] EWHC 226 [179]*

22 *Wardlaw v Bonnington Castings [1956] AC 613* [623]

23 Wilsher v Essex Area Health Authority [1988] 2 W.L.R. 557

24 Gregg v Scott No. [2005] UKHL 2 [77]

> *"The use of the word "substantial" also seems to connote a higher causative potency than Lord Reid's in excess of de minimis. The word "substantial" has also appeared in the language of others since Wardlaw's case. Examples are Lord Hoffmann in Gregg v Scott [2005] 2 AC 176, para 77 in dealing with Wilsher's case [1988] AC 1074, where he said that "The defendant was only liable if the lack of oxygen caused or substantially [my italics] contributed to the injury". This is also the language used by Lord Simon of Glaisdale in McGhee's case [1973] 1 WLR 1, 8 d.*[25]

A more pragmatic position is that of Lord Phillips in *Sienkiewicz "I doubt whether it is ever possible to define, in quantitative terms, what for the purposes of the application of any principle of law, is de minimis. This must be a question for the judge on the facts of the particular case"*[26].

<u>Chapter Summary</u>

i. The starting point for the analysis of causation in any case should be the consideration of whether standard 'but for' causation principles apply.

ii. Whether applying standard causation or material causation, findings of fact will be based on the evidence and burden is upon the claimant to prove all aspects of their case on the balance of probabilities. As confirmed by Jay J in the case of *Heneghan*:

> *"In a case where medical causation is in issue, strict adherence to logic and principle would demand proof on the balance of probabilities either of the whole of the damage suffered or of a material part of it. For these*

Bailey v MOD [2009] 1 WLR 1052 [41]

26 *Sienkiewicz v Grief (UK) Ltd [2011] UKSC 10 [108]*

> *purposes, there is no distinction between the whole and the part, provided that the part is significant*"[27]

iii. An appreciation of the causative potency of a particular agent is likely to require an understanding of the aetiology of a particular disease or injury. It is likely that as medical science evolves, the understanding of the causes of diseases will reveal more about the relationship between diseases and their causative agents.

iv. To be a causative agent, it much be proved on the balance of probabilities to have causative potential.

v. The test for whether a causative agent then reaches the threshold for being more than de minimis is likely to be factually dependent.

[27] *Heneghan v Manchester Dry Docks Ltd & Others [2016] EWCA Civ 86 [51]*

CHAPTER TWO

CATEGORIES OF DISEASE AND INJURY

Before exploring the relevant case law in detail, it is helpful to consider the approach that the courts have taken to the categorisation of disease and injury. This has informed how they have made their findings in relation to material contribution. A key recurring concept is that of divisibility.

*In Sienkiewicz, t*he Supreme Court was concerned with the applicability of *Section 3 of the Compensation Act 2006* in a case of mesothelioma. Lord Phillips undertook an analysis of causation thereby identifying categories of disease based on an analysis of their aetiology[28]:

i. **Indivisible injuries**. Lord Phillips used the example of malaria which is contracted through the inoculation by a mosquito. He described the disease process as a "*single, uniform, trigger*" with no dose variability or cumulative injury. In terms of the risk of contracting the disease he stated, "*The extent of the risk of getting malaria will depend upon the quantity of malarial mosquitoes to which the individual is exposed, but this factor will not affect the manner in which the disease is contracted nor the severity of the disease once it is contracted*". Lord Phillips went on to confirm that where a disease is indivisible, a defendant who has tortiously contributed to the cause of the disease will be liable in full[29].

---

[28] *Sienkiewicz v Grief (UK) Ltd [2011] UKSC 10 [12-15]*

[29] *Sienkiewicz v Grief (UK) Ltd [2011] UKSC 10 [90]*

ii. **Divisible Injuries.** "*More commonly, diseases where the contraction is dose related are divisible. The agent ingested operates cumulatively first to cause the disease and then to progress the disease. Thus, the severity of the disease is related to the quantity of the agent that is ingested*". Lord Phillips included in this category diseases such as asbestosis, silicosis, and injuries such as vibration white finger and industrial deafness, the severity of which increases cumulatively with the dosage of the causative agent. In terms of liability Lord Phillips confirmed that w*here* the disease is divisible the tortfeasor will be liable in respect of the share of the disease for which he is responsible[30].

iii. **Threshold Injuries.** Lord Phillips distinguished diseases such as lung cancer caused smoking whereby the contraction of the disease is dose related but following contraction, the disease may then be characterised as indivisible, *"Ingestion of the agent that causes the disease operates cumulatively so that, after a threshold is passed, it causes the onset of the disease... The severity of the disease, once it has been initiated, is not related to the degree of exposure to cigarette smoke"*.

The accuracy of Lord Phillip's characterization of lung cancer as the result of a cumulative ingestion process surpassing a threshold has not been confirmed in other cases. In *Jones*[31], claimants brought actions for various types of cancers and respiratory disease that they alleged to have been caused or materially contributed to by carcinogenic substances that they were exposed to during the course of their employment. The parties produced expert evidence on the likely cause of the injuries. Having undertaken a detailed assessment of the evidence Swift J stated:

30 *Ibid [90]*

31 *Jones v Secretary of State for Energy and Climate Change [2012] EWHC 2936 (QB)*

> *"I question whether the term "cumulative" can really be applied to the part played by the claimants' occupational exposure to carcinogens when taken in conjunction with their exposure to the carcinogens contained in cigarette smoke and with the other factors that might have played a part in the development of their cancers. In respect of a cancer suffered by any individual claimant, the occupational carcinogen might or might not have contributed and, if it did contribute, it might have played a very minor or an extremely major role. Moreover, other factors – smoking-related, environmental, and endogenous – might have been the sole cause of the cancer, might have played no part in its development or might have played a more minor or a more major role than the individual's occupational exposure to carcinogens. To describe the action of an individual claimant's occupational exposure to carcinogens as one of a number of "cumulative causes" of his cancer does not seem to me accurately to represent its role"*[32]

Swift J went on to comment:

> *"It is a very different situation from Bonnington, where the additional dust exposure caused by the defendant's breach of duty plainly had a cumulative effect by adding to the claimant's total dust exposure or from Bailey, where there was clear medical evidence that the defendant's negligence had added to the claimant's weakness which had in turn resulted in her cardiac arrest and consequent brain damage"*[33]

Swift J concluded that it was not appropriate to approach cases involving cancer by applying the principle set out in *Bonnington Castings*. One of the issues identified with such an approach would be that where the

---

[32] *Jones v Secretary of State for Energy and Climate Change [2012] EWHC 2936 (QB) [8.54]*

[33] *Ibid [8.54]*

claimant could establish tortious exposure to a carcinogen that was more than minimal, the defendant would be 100% liable in damages. Swift J expressed sympathy for claimants who find themselves struggling to establish a causative link between exposure and disease but found on balance that applying material contribution to such cases would lead to injustice for defendants.

Divisibility and indivisibility

It should be noted that the terms divisibility and indivisibility have been inconsistently applied to by the courts to describe the disease or injury process but also its outcome (see *Divisibility and Indivisibility As Sources of Confusion*)

A divisible Injury or disease

Divisibility denotes the ability of something to be divided. Ordinarily divisible injuries are also dose-related injuries. The severity of a divisible injury or dose related injury thereby varies according to the dose of the causative agent. An increase in the dose relates to an individual's exposure to the causative agent. An increase in the exposure to a causative agent corresponds to an increase in the severity of the injury or disease. Increased exposure is often gauged as the length of time an individual has been exposed to the causative agent increases the dose of that agent and the harm to that individual. The designation of a particular injury or disease as divisible requires a scientific understanding of that particular diseases process or aetiology.

In the context of occupational disease, an example of a divisible or dose related injury is industrial deafness. The causative agent is the noise that an individual has been exposed to. Damage to the mechanism of the ears is understood to increase with greater exposure to the noise. An example of a divisible or dose related disease is asbestosis, a lung disease caused by exposure to asbestos mesothelioma (*Sienkiewicz*[34]and *Fairchild*[35]). The relationship between the exposure to the agent and extent of the injury may not be linear, but broadly, a person who has had less exposure will be less affected.

In the context of clinical negligence, an example of a divisible or dose related injury is hypoxic ischemia caused by asphyxia at the time of birth (*CNZ*[36]). The greater the period of time over which the asphyxia operates, the greater the amount of hypoxic ischemia.

<u>An indivisible Injury or disease</u>

Indivisible injuries or diseases in material contribution are not dose dependent. This is irrespective of whether the term is applied to the process or the overall outcome of the injury or disease. They are caused by the "*single, uniform, trigger*"[37]as described by Lord Phillips in *Sienkiewicz*. The relationship between the causative agent and the extent of the injury or disease is unrelated to the dose that individual has been exposed to. It is binary: either an individual has the injury, or they do not.

An example of an indivisible injury would be a fracture. An example of an indivisible disease would be mesothelioma, a cancer caused by exposure to asbestos. Indivisible injuries like cancer require exposure to the causative agent, but the relationship between the exposure and the cancer is less clear cut. An individual will not get more cancer the greater the dose of the exposure to the causative agents. Once an indivisible

---

34 *Sienkiewicz v Grief (UK) Ltd [2011] UKSC 10*

Fairchild v Glenhaven [2002] UKHL 22

36 *CNZ (Suing By Her Father and Litigation Friend MNZ) v Royal Bath Hospitals NHS Foundation Trust and Another [2023] EWHC 19 (KB)*

37 *Sienkiewicz v Grief (UK) Ltd [2011] UKSC 10 [12]*

disease has been triggered, the disease runs its own discrete course unrelated to the dosage or exposure.

The concept of divisibility or indivisibility has been retrospectively applied by the courts in their attempts to analyze cases (see *Subsequent analysis of Bonnington Castings*[38]). Also note the comments made by Swift J in *Jones*[39] (set out above).

A cumulative Injury or disease.

The term cumulative refers to a disease or injury process that occurs by the additive effect of the causative agents. Where a cumulative injury has been caused by an individual's exposure to one causative agent the injury may be analogous to a dose dependent divisible injury. Other cumulative injuries or diseases may describe the cumulative effect of various distinct causative agents and not necessarily be dose dependent. An example of this would be the cumulative effect of a fall, a period of raised intracranial pressure, and a post-operative infection on the claimant's brain injury as occurred in the case of *John*[40].

Alternatively, a cumulative injury may be the result of a threshold being surmounted. The 'heart attack' (myocardial ischemia) suffered by the claimant in *Williams*[41] may best be described as a cumulative injury: a cumulative divisible injury process (sepsis) causing an indivisible outcome (heart attack). The notion of a cumulative injury does not conform precisely to the notions of indivisibility and divisibility.

---

38 *Wardlaw v Bonnington Castings [1956] AC 613* [623]

39 *Jones v Secretary of State for Energy and Climate Change [2012] EWHC 2936 (QB) [8.54]*

40 *Dr Sido John v Central Manchester and Manchester Children's University Hospitals NHS Foundation Trust [2016] EWHC 407 (QB)*

41 *Williams v The Bermuda Hospitals Board [2016] UKPC [32]*

Divisibility and Indivisibility As Sources of Confusion

The extent of the confusion within the jurisprudence of material contribution is alluded to by HHJ Auerbach in *Davies*:

"One of the hazards when seeking to interpret the discussion in the later authorities, is that labels like "material contribution" and "cumulative cause case" are not always used in the same sense. Their use does not necessarily signify that the Court is contemplating that some such additional route to liability may be, or does, apply... Sometimes what is meant is less than clear"[42]

Divisibility and indivisibility have become key constructs in the courts' analysis of the facts in cases where material contribution has been plead. The terms have however been inconsistently applied. A particular source of confusion has been the use of the term 'indivisible'. When applied to the injury or disease *process*, indivisibility readily conforms to the definition as set out above. An indivisible disease *process* such as that which may occur in cancer or malaria, is the opposite of a divisible injury or disease *process*.

The term indivisible has, however, also been used to describe the *outcome* of an injury or disease. In that context, indivisibility has been used as a term to describe the inability of medical science to clearly distinguish the precise the cause of the *outcome*. The totality of an injury or disease may be described as indivisible insofar as the operation of its constituent components or causative agents are indistinguishable. An example of this use of the term 'indivisible' occurs in the judgment of the Privy Council in *Williams*. In the context of these two uses of the term indivisible, various diseases and injuries may be capable of being described as both divisible and indivisible depending upon whether it is the *process* or the *outcome* that is being described.

A final source of confusion in terms of divisibility of indivisibility has occurred where the terms are used in the context of apportioning

42 *Davies v Frimley Health NHS Foundation Trust [2021] EWHC 169 [202]*

damages against each contributing tortfeasor (as distinct from describing causation in respect of a disease or injury). This arguably is the context in which divisibility was applied in *AB*[43]. In *Davies* HHJ Auerbach re-framed material contribution as the exercise by which a court apportions damage amongst co-contributors as follows:

> "*First, where the harm is divisible, a party will be liable if their culpable conduct made a contribution to the harm, to the extent of that contribution. Secondly, where the harm is indivisible, a party will be liable for the whole of it, if they caused it, applying "but for" principles. Thirdly, if two wrongdoers have both together caused an indivisible injury, in respect of which it is impossible to apportion liability between them, then each is co-liable for the whole of the injury suffered. This approach may, at least in some sub-permutations, be seen as a modification of the "but for" test, but it is doctrinally well-established and accepted…I call these the orthodox routes to liability*"[44].

Divisibility and Indivisibility As Applied To Cases.

In *Bonnington Castings* the pneumoconiosis disease was found to have been caused by the inhalation of dust to which the defendant had made a material contribution. Subsequent analysis by the courts has questioned whether the pneumoconiosis was being treated by the House of Lords as a divisible or as an indivisible injury.

Referring to *Bonnington Castings* in *Sienkiewicz,* Lord Phillips stated:

> *"That disease is divisible. The severity of the disease depends upon the quantity of silica inhaled. The defendant did not, however, argue that, if held liable, this should only be to the extent that the dust for which it was responsible had contributed*

43 *AB v Ministry of Defence [2010] EWCA Civ 131*

44 *Davies v Frimley Health NHS Foundation Trust [2021] EWHC 169 [200]*

> *to the plaintiff's symptoms. It was held liable for 100% of the disease. There have, however, been a series of cases at first instance and in the Court of Appeal in which it has been recognised that where there has been a number of exposures of a claimant to bodily insults that have cumulatively caused a divisible disease, responsibility should be apportioned so that an individual defendant is liable for no more than his share of the disease. This apportionment may necessarily be a rough and ready exercise"*[45]

Bonnington Castings has been cited as an authority for the principle that material contribution can apply to divisible dose related injuries or diseases and that having established divisibility this should then allow for the apportionment between the negligent and non-negligent causative agents. Does that principle apply to divisible injuries and diseases to the exclusion of those that have been described as indivisible?

This appeared to be the opinion of Smith LJ as stated in the Court of Appeal case of *AB*. She stated that the principle in *Bonnington Castings* "*applies only where the disease or condition is 'divisible' so that an increased dose of the harmful agent worsens the disease*" [46]. Smith LJ went on to described *Bailey*[47] (a Court of Appeal case on which she sat) as another divisible injury type case.

In *Williams*[48], the Privy Council considered that because of the way that the pneumoconiosis disease in *Bonnington Castings* was presented, the House of Lords were effectively considering an indivisible disease. On that interpretation, it was therefore the indivisible nature of the pneumoconiosis that led to the claimant recovering on a 100% basis.

45 *Sienkiewicz v Grief (UK) Ltd [2011] UKSC 10 [17]*

46 *AB v Ministry of Defence [2010] EWCA Civ. 1317[150]*

47 *Bailey v MOD [2009] 1 WLR 1052 [41]*

48 *Williams v The Bermuda Hospitals Board [2016] UKPC [32]*

Similarly in the case of *Bailey*, there was no suggestion that the ultimate brain injury suffered by the claimant was divisible. Rather it was the weakness that led to the brain injury that was potentially divisible. In the High Court case of *Rich*, Jay J commented:

> "*it would be much neater...to say that the Defendant's tort contributed to the mechanism which led to Ms Bailey's indivisible injury or injuries*" [49]

CNZ was heard in the High Court before Ritchie J. The judgment contains an analysis of divisibility in the context of the claimant sustaining a brain injury at birth:

> "*An indivisible disease is one which starts when triggered and then goes on and gets worse or takes its course whatever the exposure to the noxious substance after the triggering event. These diseases are not divisible in the sense that they are not reduced by stopping the exposure and do not get worse on increasing the exposure. They start and then they progress, like cancer or mesothelioma*"[50].

The judge concluded that the process of brain injury sustained by the claimant was divisible and "*wholly dose dependent*" but which led to a functional outcome that could not be apportioned.

---

49 *Miss Melissa Rich (A Protected Party by Her Mother and Litigation Friend Helen Rich) v Hull and East Yorkshire Hospitals NHS Trust [2015] EWHC 3395 [205]*

50 *CNZ (Suing By Her Father and Litigation Friend MNZ) v Royal Bath Hospitals NHS Foundation Trust and Another [2023] EWHC 19 (KB) [361]*

The recent judgments in the clinical negligence cases of *Davies*[51] and *Thorley*[52] following the judgments of the Court of Appeal in *AB*[53] and *Heneghan*[54] affirmed that material contribution can only apply to divisible injuries. These later decisions have thereby cast doubt over the application of material contribution and created uncertainty as to the future applicability of material contribution. As stated by Soole J in *Thorley* "*This is evidently a legal issue which is ripe for authoritative review, at least in a case where it may affect the result*" [55]

Part of any review would be to clarify whether certain classes of disease and injury exist to which material contribution causation cannot apply. There is a natural association between a lack of scientific understanding of a disease or injury and its potential indivisibility. It is conceivable that despite expert evidence many disease and injury processes will not be comprehended to the extent that they can be characterised as divisible and all the potential causative components, cumulative. It is no doubt in the interests of justice that a disease process is found to be divisible so as to apportion between tortfeasors. To exclude other diseases or injuries on the basis that they cannot be divided and apportioned may lead to injustice.

<u>Chapter Summary</u>

i. The question of whether a disease or injury is divisible, or indivisible is often a central consideration in the determination of whether material contribution can be applied.

---

[51] *v Frimley Health NHS Foundation Trust [2021] EWHC 169*

[52] *Thorley v Sandwell and West Birmingham NHS Trust [2021] EWHC 2604*

[53] *AB v Ministry of Defence [2010] EWCA Civ 131*

[54] *Heneghan v Manchester Dry Docks Ltd & Others [2016] EWCA Civ 86*

[55] *Thorley v Sandwell and West Birmingham NHS Trust [2021] EWHC 2604 [151]*

ii. An injury or disease may have characteristics that can be described as both divisible and indivisible depending upon whether the terms are being applied to the disease process or to the outcome.

iii. Where a disease or injury is considered divisible, the courts will attempt to apportion the damages according to the extent of a defendant's responsibility.

iv. In *Davies* and *Thorley*, the courts considered that they were bound by the decisions of the Court of Appeal in *AB* and *Heneghan* on the matter of divisibility in the context of material contribution.

PART ONE

ORIGINS OF MATERIAL CONTRIBUTION IN OCCUPATIONAL DISEASE

As a necessary prelude to exploring material contribution in clinical negligence cases, it is important to understand the way the courts have considered the relation between negligence and disease in the context of occupational disease. The judgments in most clinical negligence cases are reasoned with reference to occupational disease jurisprudence.

Occupational disease claims are brought by employees against employers in relation to various categories of disease. Examples include pneumoconiosis (*Bonnington Castings*[56]) dermatitis (*McGhee*[57]), industrial deafness (*Thompson*[58]), asbestosis (Holtby[59]), mesothelioma (*Sienkiewicz*[60] *and Fairchild*[61]) and cancers (*Heneghan*[62] *and AB*[63]). In

56 *Wardlaw v Bonnington Castings [1956] AC 613*

57 *McGhee v National Coal Board 1973 S.C. (H.L.) 37*

58 *Thompson v Smiths Shiprepairers (North Shields) Ltd [1984] QB 405*

59 Holtby v Brigham & Cowan (Hull) Ltd [2000 WL 345159]

60 *Sienkiewicz v Grief (UK) Ltd [2011] UKSC 10*

61 *Fairchild v Glenhaven [2002] UKHL 22*

62 *Heneghan v Manchester Dry Docks Ltd & Others [2016] EWCA Civ 86*

63 *AB v Ministry of Defence [2010] EWCA Civ 131*

analyzing causation has the courts have relied upon medical experts to understand the mode by which disease is contracted and develops.

Commonly in occupational disease cases, an individual will have developed a medical condition having been exposed to a single causative agent while in the course of their employment. In the cases involving asbestos for example, the claimant may advance a claim for asbestosis or mesothelioma often having worked for several employers over the course of their working life thereby exposing them to the same causative agent from different origins. It is trite law in negligence that a tortfeasor should only be required to compensate to the extent of their liability. Employers will therefore reasonably seek to limit their liability to the proportion of the losses that they consider themselves to be responsible for.

Whilst considering the applicability of occupational disease cases to clinical negligence, it is important to be aware of the role of policy arguments. Lord Bingham in *Fairchild* justified the modification of the standard test for causation in cases of industrial disease:

> "*strong policy argument in favour of compensating those who have suffered grave harm, at the expense of their employers who owed them a duty to protect them against that very harm and failed to do so, when the harm can only have been caused by breach of that duty and when science does not permit the victim accurately to attribute, as between several employers, the precise responsibility for the harm he has suffered*"[64]

64 *Fairchild v Glenhaven [2002] UKHL 22 [33]*

CHAPTER THREE

A SINGLE CAUSATIVE AGENT FROM TWO SOURCES

Wardlaw v Bonnington Castings [1956] AC 613

In considering material contribution cases brought in clinical negligence the courts have consistently returned to the findings in *Bonnington Castings*. Lord Rodger in *Fairchild* contended that "*the idea of liability based on wrongful conduct that had materially contributed to an injury was … well established long before Wardlaw. But Wardlaw became a convenient point of reference, especially in cases of industrial disease*"[65]

The claimant, a steel dresser, brought a claim against his employer on the grounds that he had contracted pneumoconiosis through their negligence and breach of statutory duty. The claimant had worked for years with his face near a "*pneumatic hammer*" that had released particles of silica dust. Inhalation of silica dust was understood to be dangerous and a cause of pneumoconiosis. The area in which the claimant worked also contained other equipment referred to as "*swing grinders*" that also emitted silica dust.

The swing grinders were fitted with dust extraction units which the defendant admitted were inadequate. There was however no method available at the time for extracting the dust from the pneumatic hammer. The defendant argued that the danger to the claimant was from the dust inhaled due to his proximity to the pneumatic hammer as opposed to the dust from the swing grinders.

---

[65] *Fairchild v Glenhaven [2002] UKHL 22 [129]*

The defendant further argued that the burden was upon the claimant to demonstrate that the pneumoconiosis had been caused by the dust resulting from their admitted failures. It was the defendant's position that some of the dust had been created through negligence but that the claimant needed to prove that but for the negligent dust, he would not have contacted pneumoconiosis "*the pursuer had not been able to connect his injury with the inadequately protected swing grinders*"[66]

The case was heard before the Court of Session who found the defendant liable for damages on the basis that their negligence had caused or materially contributed to the pneumoconiosis. The defendant appealed to the Inner House who upheld the decision against the defendant holding that the burden was on the employer to disprove that the dust from the swing grinders had contributed to the disease. Lord Precedent Clyde dissented. He considered that the claimant had burden of proving causation. The case was heard before the House of Lords in January 1956.

The principal judgment was given by Lord Reid. He agreed with Lord Clyde that the claimant was required to prove on the balance of probabilities that his disease was caused or materially contributed to from his having inhaled part of the noxious dust from the swing grinders.

> "*In my judgment, the employee must in all cases prove his case by the ordinary standard of proof in civil actions: he must make it appear at least that on a balance of probabilities the breach of duty caused or materially contributed to his injury.*"[67]

In terms of the causal role of silica dust in pneumoconiosis, Lord Reid stated:

---

66 *Wardlaw v Bonnington Castings [1956] AC 613 [27]*

67 *Wardlaw v Bonnington Castings [1956] AC 613 [31]*

> "*The medical evidence was that pneumoconiosis is caused by a gradual accumulation in the lungs of minute particles of silica inhaled over a period of years. That means, I think, that the disease is caused by the whole of the noxious material inhaled and, if that material comes from two sources, it cannot be wholly attributed to material from one source or the other*"[68]

Lord Reid further clarified his position in relation to causation:

> "*I am in agreement with much of the Lord President's opinion in this case, but I cannot agree that the question is which was the most probable source of the respondent's disease, the dust from the pneumatic hammers or the dust from the swing grinders. It appears to me that the source of his disease was the dust from both sources, and the real question is whether the dust from the swing grinders materially contributed to the disease*"[69]

In terms of the silica dust, Lord Reid considered that only a more than minimal contribution needed to be made by the negligent swing grinders to the disease process to enable the claimant to succeed in respect of his entire injury . Lord Reid described the proportion of dust emanated from the swing grinders as having material contributed to the overall amount of dust that the claimant would have inhaled. The so-called "*guilty dust*" was indivisible from the "*innocent dust*" both of which materially contribution the injury.

Approving the judgment, Lord Keith commented on the mode by which the silica particles acted upon the claimant. He described the pneumoconiosis as:

> "*a disease of gradual incidence. Small though the contribution of pollution may be for which the defenders are to blame, it was*

68 Ibid [31]

69 Ibid [31]

> *continuous over a long period. In cumulo it must have been substantial, though it might remain small in proportion... Prima facie the particles inhaled are acting cumulatively, and I think the natural inference is that had it not been for the cumulative effect the pursuer would not have developed pneumoconiosis when he did and might not have developed it at all"*[70]

Subsequent analysis of Bonnington Castings

The above passage from the judgment of Lord Keith characterised a cumulative process resonant of a dose related disease process. His comments were made in the context of the defendant being unable to prove that their negligence did not cause the injury: absent the negligent dust, the claimant might not have developed pneumoconiosis at all. Waller J giving judgment in *Bailey* considered that Lord Keith's language "*could be said to support a "but for" approach*" to causation[71]

Giving judgment on behalf of the Privy Council in *Williams*, Lord Toulson noted that in *Bonnington Castings*:

> "*there was no suggestion that the pneumoconiosis was 'divisible', meaning that the severity of the disease depended on the quantity of dust inhaled. Lord Reid interpreted the medical evidence as meaning that the particles from the swing grinders were a cause of the entire disease. True, they were only part of the cause, but they were a partial cause of the entire injury, as distinct from being a cause of only part of the injury"*[72]

Lord Toulson thereby sought to characterise the injury in *Bonnington Castings* as assessed by the House of Lords to be an indivisible injury. The

70 Ibid [36]

71 *Bailey v MOD [2009] 1 WLR 1052* [40]

72 *Williams v The Bermuda Hospitals Board [2016] UKPC [32]*

footnotes to the judgment in *Williams* note in relation to *Bonnington Castings*:

> *"In later cases it has been the accepted view that pneumoconiosis is a "divisible" disease, its severity being dependent on the quantity of dust inhaled; and, therefore, where there has been more than one source of toxic material, the extent of the liability of a defendant responsible for part of the exposure should reflect the degree of injury suffered by the claimant as a result of that exposure"*[73]

In contrast, Lord Phillips in *Sienkiewicz* characterised *Bonnington Castings* as a case of a divisible injury to which apportionment could theoretically have been applied had the issue been raised by the defendant.

Also giving judgment in *Sienkiewicz*, Lady Hale characterised the findings in *Bonnington Castings* as a cumulative injury case where the defendant had made a more than minimal contribution to the development of the condition. She agreed with Lord Phillips that the claimant's recovery on an 100% basis was a consequence of the defendant taking no point on apportionment, making the following observations:

> *"in a series of subsequent such cases damages have been apportioned, however broadly – for example, as between negligent and non-negligent exposure respectively in dust inhalation cases, in noise cases and in cases of vibration white finger, and, in respiratory disease cases, between the damage caused by the inhalation of fumes or other noxious agents on the one hand and the claimant's habit of cigarette smoking on the other"*[74]

73 *Williams v The Bermuda Hospitals Board [2016] UKPC [Footnote]*

74 *Sienkiewicz v Grief (UK) Ltd [2011] UKSC 10 [176]*

The same position was taken by Smith LJ in the case of *AB*:

> "*At no stage in that case [Bonnington Castings] was it suggested that the damages should be apportioned as between the effect of the tortious and non-tortious components. If that had been suggested, and if expert evidence had been called showing the effect of the different components (as we think it would be nowadays), the damages would probably have been apportioned. The plaintiff would have recovered damages for only the harm caused by the tort and there would have been no need for any modification of the 'but for' rule*"[75]

Smith LJ went on to state that the causation principle of material contribution as defined in *Bonnington Castings* could only be applied where the disease or condition was divisible in the sense that an increased dose of the harmful agent worsens the disease. This proposition regarding the test in *Bonnington Castings* was confirmed in the judgment in *Heneghan*:

> [*The Bonnington test]* "*... is to be applied where the court is satisfied on scientific evidence that the exposure for which the defendant is responsible has in fact contributed to the injury. This is readily demonstrated in the case of divisible injuries (such as silicosis and pneumoconiosis) whose severity is proportionate to the amount of exposure to the causative agent*"[76]

The divisibility of the injury was not a matter that was before the court in *Bonnington Castings* and as such the case was not decided with reference to divisibility. The differences in opinion as to whether the injury in Bonnington Castings was indivisible or divisible and whether

---

75 *AB v Ministry of Defence [2010] EWCA Civ 131* [134]

76 *Heneghan v Manchester Dry Docks Ltd & Others [2016] EWCA Civ 86 [46]*

this defines the application of material contribution are unlikely to be resolved without guidance from the Supreme Court.

Chapter Summary

i. *Bonnington Castings* was a single causative agent case. The agent was dust. The conundrum was that it came from two sources. There was no issue with the claimant proving that the dust was on the balance of probabilities responsible for the injury.

ii. The House of Lords confirmed material contribution as a method of proving causation where attribution could be not be discerned between two sources of the same causative agent.

iii. The Privy Council in *Williams* interpreted *Bonnington Castings* as an authority for the principle that material contribution causation could be applied to an indivisible disease. The interpretation in *Sienkiewicz* and *AB* was that the House of Lords were applying material contribution to a divisible injury.

CHAPTER FOUR

MATERIAL CONTRIBUTION TO THE RISK

The concept of a material increase in risk originated in the cases of *Nicholson*[77] and *McGhee*[78]. In *Bonnington Castings* it was found that the dust, whether of negligent or non-negligent origin, was on the balance of probabilities the likely cause of the claimant's pneumoconiosis. The task for the court in *Bonnington Castings* was therefore to consider whether the defendant could be found liable for their contribution to the disease itself.

Where there exists an association between a causative agent and the injury, but it is not possible to say on the balance of probabilities whether the causative agent itself caused the injury , the courts have on occasion inferred the existence of an increase in the risk of causing the injury to bridge the evidential gap.

Nicholson v Atlas [1957] 1 W.L.R 613

The year after the Bonnington Castings case was heard, another Scottish case based on similar facts was considered by The House of Lords. The claimant was again a steel dresser who had been employed operating pneumatic hammers. He had contracted pneumoconiosis from the inhalation of silica dust. The case brought by his family was that the factory had breached their duty of care by failing to provide adequate ventilation in the factory. The court of first instance dismissed the case. This was then reversed by the First Division of the Court of Session before being appealed to the House of Lords. The decisions of the lower

77 *Nicholson v Atlas [1957] 1 W.L.R 613*

78 *McGhee v National Coal Board [1973] 1 WLR 1*

courts had been made before the decision of the House of Lords in *Bonnington Castings* had been handed down.

One nuance of the facts in *Nicholson* was that there was no clear distinction between the dust from different sources. The central alleged breach was in relation to the ventilation of the factory space. On that basis the claimant argued that it was the prolonged exposure to the dust that had materially contributed to the pneumoconiosis. As states by *Viscount Simmonds:*

> *"It is admitted by the respondents that the deceased inhaled while in their employment the particles which caused his illness and ultimately his death, but they contend that it was not proved that particles which were wrongfully emitted, or which, having been innocently emitted, were allowed, through inadequate ventilation, to remain within his breathing zone, made a material contribution to his illness"*[79]

The House of Lords felt obliged to apply the test in *Bonnington Castings* and found for the claimant. However, contained within the judgment of Viscount Simmonds there is reference to the defendant's negligence increasing the "*risk*" of injury to the claimant:

> *"It follows that owing to the default of the respondents the deceased was exposed to a greater degree of risk than he should have been, and, though it is impossible, even approximately, to quantify the particles which he must, in any event, have inhaled and those which he inhaled but need not have, I cannot regard the excess as something so negligible that the maxim "de minimis" is applicable. Accordingly, following the decision in Wardlaw's case, I must hold the respondents liable"*[80]

---

79 *Nicholson v Atlas [1957] 1 W.L.R 613 [615]*

80 *Nicholson v Atlas [1957] 1 W.L.R 613 [620]*

This notion of an increase in the risk is echoed in the judgment of Lord Cohen:

> *"Pneumoconiosis is a progressive disease. The longer a workman is exposed to an intense cloud the graver must be the risk of infection...It seems to me to follow that the respondents' failure to provide adequate ventilation must increase the risk to which the workmen are exposed. Reading the evidence as a whole, I think it establishes that (to use the language of Lord Reid in Wardlaw's case "on a balance of probabilities the breach of duty caused or materially contributed to" the injury"*[81]

McGhee v National Coal Board [1973 S.C. (H.L.) 37]

In *McGee* the House of Lords developed the proposition in *Nicholson* to reformulate material contribution causation and create a material increase in risk test.

The claimant was a laborer at a brickworks. During his daily employment, he would become covered in dust. The Claimant was moved from the pipe kilns to the brick kilns which were accepted to have been dustier than the pipe kilns. Having worked in the brick kilns for a few days, the Claimant developed occupational dermatitis from his exposure to the dust and sued his employer for inter alia failing to provide adequate washing facilities to remove the dust at the end of the day.

The Lord Ordinary found the defendant to be at fault for not providing washing facilities but found the claimant to have failed to prove a causal connection between the 10 to 15-minute period between leaving work and arriving at home (where there existed facilities to wash), and the development of the dermatitis. The height of the medical evidence was that washing would have materially reduced the risk of contracting dermatitis. Washing would not on the balance of probabilities have prevented the dermatitis. The negligence simply exposed the claimant to

81 Ibid [622]

the dust for 10 to 15 minutes longer. The court of the First Division agreed with the reasoning of the lower court.

The key question for the House of Lords was whether the defendant could be found liable for failing to reduce the risk to the claimant of contracting dermatitis by failing to provide washing facilities. The defendant argued that the washing facilities would not have eliminated the risk and therefore the claimant may have developed dermatitis in any event. The defendant sought to distinguish *Bonnington Castings* on the basis that in that case the dust particles were responsible for the causing the pneumoconiosis rather than simply culpable of increasing the risk.

The key findings of Lord Reid's lead judgment can be summarised as follows:

i. The dust caused the dermatitis through a cumulative process "*the longer a subject is exposed to injury the greater the chance of his developing dermatitis*"[82]

ii. The process by which the dust caused the dermatitis was different from the way the dust caused pneumoconiosis in *Bonnington Castings* "*It may be that an accumulation of minor abrasions of the horny layer of the skin is a necessary precondition for the onset of the disease*"[83]

iii. The period over which the dust was in contact with the claimant's skin was causative of the dermatitis "*I cannot accept the view…that once the man left the brick kiln he left behind the causes which made him liable to develop dermatitis*"[84]

[82] *McGhee v National Coal Board [1973] 1 WLR 1[52]*

[83] Ibid [53]

[84] Ibid [44]

Lord Reid made no distinction between a material increase in the risk of dermatitis and making a material contribution to the occurrence of dermatitis:

> "*it has often been said that the legal concept of causation is not based on logic or philosophy. It is based on the practical way in which the ordinary man's mind works in the everyday affairs of life. From a broad and practical viewpoint, I can see no substantial difference between saying that what the defender did materially increased the risk of injury to the pursuer and saying that what the defender did made a material contribution to his injury*"[85]

This finding was echoed by Lord Simon who considered "*material reduction of the risk*" and "*substantial contribution to the injury*" to be "*mirror concepts*"[86]. Similarly, Lord Salmon stated "*it seems to me unrealistic and contrary to ordinary common sense to hold that the negligence which materially increased the risk of injury did not materially contribute to causing the injury.*"[87]

Lord Salmon went on state:

> "*In the circumstances of the present case, the possibility of a distinction existing between (a) having materially increased the risk of contracting the disease, and (b) having materially contributed to causing the disease may no doubt be a fruitful source of interesting academic discussions between students of philosophy. Such a distinction is, however, far too unreal to be recognised by the common law*"[88]

85 Ibid [54]

86 Ibid [57]

87 Ibid [61]

88 Ibid [62]

The House of Lords found for the claimant on causation. Apportionment was not considered as it had been the defendant's case that they were not liable at all. The majority favoured dropping the test from material contribution to the disease to material contribution to the risk of suffering the disease. Lord Kilbrandon considered that on the balance of probabilities the lack of washing had caused the disease.

Subsequent analysis of McGhee

Analysis by the courts has considered that rather than simply applying *Bonnington Castings*, the court in McGhee effectively extended the test for material contribution. As stated by Jay J in the case of *Heneghan*:

> *"He (Lord Reid) recognised that in the earlier case (Bonnington Castings) it was proved that every particle of dust played its part in the onset of the disease. Given the current state of expert knowledge, that could not be said in McGhee. However, a "broader view of causation" [page 4G/H], and the equation of material contribution to the damage with material contribution to the risk, led to the same conclusion. So, it was only in McGhee that we see the equation in Lord Reid's mind between these two concepts"*[89]

Fairchild v Glenhaven Funeral Services *[2002] UKHL 22*

The House of Lords in Fairchild was asked to consider whether the test for material contribution of risk could be deployed to assist claimants who had contracted mesothelioma during the course of their employment by several employers.

Mesothelioma is a cancer that is contracted when an individual inhales fibres of asbestos. It was understood that it could potentially be caused by the inhalation of a single fibre which can set up inflammation in the lung leading to the development of mesothelioma many years later.

---

89 *Heneghan v Manchester Dry Docks Ltd & Others [2016] EWCA Civ 86 [52]*

Medical science was unable to distinguish which fibre caused the disease, but the more fibres inhaled, the greater risk to that individual of developing the condition. The risk of developing mesothelioma was therefore likely related to the dose of asbestos that the individual was exposed to in his working life. The disease once triggered was however not dose related.

It was accepted that the defendants had wrongly exposed the claimant to asbestos but argued that the claims should be dismissed because it was not possible to say on which of numerous occasions the mesothelioma had been caused. The House of Lords recognised that causation could not be established applying conventional 'but for' causation and this was an injustice to the claimants. The application of material increase in risk was accepted as the only way to bridge the gap in scientific understanding and prevent injustice for the claimant.

Lord Bingham considered that a claimant would be only able to successfully rely upon material increase in risk when six relevant factors were all present[90]:

1) C was employed at different times and for differing periods by both A and B, and

2) A and B were both subject to a duty to take reasonable care or to take all practicable measures to prevent C inhaling asbestos dust because of the known risk that asbestos dust (if inhaled) might cause a mesothelioma, and

3) Both A and B were in breach of that duty in relation to C during the periods of C's employment by each of them with the result that during both periods C inhaled excessive quantities of asbestos dust, and

90 Fairchild v Glenhaven Funeral Services [2002] UKHL 22 [2]

4) C is found to be suffering from a mesothelioma, and

5) any cause of C's mesothelioma other than the inhalation of asbestos dust at work can be effectively discounted, but

6) C cannot (because of the current limits of human science) prove, on the balance of probabilities, that his mesothelioma was the result of his inhaling asbestos dust during his employment by A or during his employment by B or during his employment by A and B taken together,

Following *Fairchild,* Parliament enacted section 3 of the Compensation Act 2006 creating a special rule governing the attribution of causation to those responsible for exposing victims of mesothelioma to asbestos dust. The legislation enabled claimants to recover in full, from any defendant who exposed an individual diagnosed with mesothelioma to a significant quantity of asbestos dust.

Since *Fairchild*, the courts have been reluctant to extend the types of cases or diseases to which material increase in risk can be applied. A similar exception was envisaged by the claimant in the case of *AB*. In that case, Smith LJ confirmed the boundaries of *Fairchild*:

> *" .... So, we conclude that there is no foreseeable possibility that the Supreme Court would be willing to extend the Fairchild exception so as to cover conditions such as we are here concerned with, which have multiple potential causes some of which have not even been identified. We reject as highly unlikely the suggestion that the Supreme Court might be prepared, on policy grounds, to extend the exception well beyond that which was contemplated at the time of Fairchild or Barker. We say that because, to effect such a change would be to upset completely the*

> *long-established principle on which proof of causation is based...*"[91]

To date, Fairchild remains an exception confined to lung cancer caused by asbestos (see *Heneghan v Manchester Dry Docks Ltd & Others [2016] EWCA Civ 86*)

Sienkiewicz v Grief (UK) Ltd [2011] UKSC 10, 2011 WL 674961

Sienkiewicz was another case concerning mesothelioma. The Supreme Court were asked to consider the application of the Compensation Act 2006 where the occupational exposure to asbestos had been very small. The defendant argued that on the balance of probability the exposure for which they were responsible was not causative and that applying epidemiological evidence, the exposure failed to double the background risk to the claimant.

Lord Phillips confirmed that the "special rule" in causation regarding material increase in risk was devised out of an ignorance about the operation of the biological agent causative of the disease. Applying *Fairchild,* the Supreme Court found for the claimant.

Doubling of the risk test

The Doubling of risk test may be defined as an inference drawn by the court by which a claimant may succeed in establishing causation. It applies to cases concerning types of diseases and injuries which have been subject to epidemiological research. When such data has been generated, it may be statistically demonstrable that the chance or risk of event is more likely than not to occur. Standard causation principles remain applied. Doubling the risk is not directly related to material contribution

[91] *AB v Ministry of Defence [2010] EWCA Civ 131* [154]

but an argument raised in clinical negligence cases where traditional 'but for' causation cannot be established on the facts.

The concept was succinctly explained by Lord Phillips in Sienkiewicz:

> *"The "doubles the risk" test is one that applies epidemiological data to determining causation on balance of probabilities in circumstances where medical science does not permit determination with certainty of how and when an injury was caused. The reasoning goes as follows. If statistical evidence indicates that the intervention of a wrongdoer more than doubled the risk that the victim would suffer the injury, then it follows that it is more likely than not that the wrongdoer caused the injury"*[92]

Lord Phillips went on to consider whether epidemiological data and the doubling the risk test could be applied to cases of multiple causative agents. It was doubted whether the test could be applied in cases of multiple tortfeasors. The judge considered further whether the order in which an individual was exposed to potentially causative agents was relevant to the application of the test:

> *"Where the initiation of the disease is dose related, and there have been consecutive exposures to an agent or agents that cause the disease, one innocent and one tortious, the position will depend upon which exposure came first in time. Where it was the tortious exposure, it is axiomatic that this will have contributed to causing the disease, even if it is not the sole cause. Where the innocent exposure came first, there may be an issue as to whether this was sufficient to trigger the disease or whether the subsequent, tortious, exposure contributed to the cause. I can see no reason in principle why the "doubles the risk" test should not be applied in such circumstances, but the court must be*

[92] Sienkiewicz v Grief (UK) Ltd [2011] UKSC 10, 2011 WL 674961 [72]

> *astute to see that the epidemiological evidence provides a really sound basis for determining the statistical probability of the cause or causes of the disease"*[93]

In the case of *Novartis*[94], the claimant had been diagnosed with bladder cancer. In terms of potential causative agents, the claimant had tortiously been exposed to carcinogens in the course of his employment in a dye works. He had also been a regular smoker. Both were potential causes of the claimant's bladder cancer. The judge at first instance applied *Bonnington Castings* to find that the negligent exposure had made a material contribution to the cancer. The defendant appealed and successfully argued that the negligent exposure had made only a material contribution to the risk of the cancer and that this was not sufficient proof of causation. The Court of Appeal found however that the tortious exposure had more than doubled the risk arising from smoking. The court held that that was sufficient for the claim to succeed.

In *Williams* the Privy Council addressed arguments raised in relation to the finding of causation based on the doubling of the risk. Lord Toulson advocated caution where epidemiological data is deployed as evidence of causation in relation to past instances "*If it is a known fact that a particular type of act (or omission) is likely to have a particular effect, proof that the defendant was responsible for such an act (or omission) and that the claimant had what is the usual effect will be powerful evidence from which to infer causation, without necessarily requiring a detailed scientific explanation for the link. But inferring causation from proof of heightened risk is never an exercise to apply mechanistically. A doubled tiny risk will still be very small"*[95]

The evidential weight of the doubling the risk test was confirmed by the Court of Appeal in the case of *Heneghan.* The case considered the likely cause of the claimant's asbestos related lung cancer in the context of his

---

93 Sienkiewicz v Grief (UK) Ltd [2011] UKSC 10, 2011 WL 674961 [90-91]

94 *Novartis Grimsby Ltd v Cookson [2007] EWCA Civ 1261*

95 *Williams v The Bermuda Hospitals Board [2016] UKPC [48]*

having worked for the defendants for only a small proportion of entire period of exposure. The use of epidemiological evidence was confirmed by as potentially capable of determining causation on the balance of probabilities where medical science could not provide the answer as to how an injury was caused "*If statistical evidence shows that a tortfeasor more than doubled the risk that the victim would suffer the injury, it follows that it is more likely than not that the tortfeasor caused the injury*"[96]

Chapter Summary

i. In the cases of *Nicholson* and *McGhee*, the test for material contribution was fundamentally altered to a test in causation based on a material increase in risk of an injury or disease occurring.

ii. The extension of the test was in response to circumstances where the claimant was unlikely to succeed due to gaps in the evidence that science was incapable of bridging. The cases of *Fairchild* and *Barker*[97]represented the limit to which the courts were prepared to stretch causation based on public policy. The position was addressed by Parliament in enacting the Compensation Act 2006.

iii. The doubling of the risk test may apply where epidemiological evidence is adduced in support of the likelihood of a counterfactual outcome. The court in *Rich*[98] considered allegations of a failure to provide a course of corticosteroid treatment. The analysis by Jay J provides an example of the court's approach to statistical data.

---

96 *Heneghan v Manchester Dry Docks Ltd & Others [2016] EWCA Civ 86[8]*

97 *Barker v Corus (UK) plc [2006] UKHL*

98 *Miss Melissa Rich (A Protected Party by Her Mother and Litigation Friend Helen Rich) v Hull and East Yorkshire Hospitals NHS Trust [2015] EWHC 3395*

CHAPTER FIVE

RECENT OCCUPATIONAL DISEASE CASES CONSIDERING MATERIAL CONTRIBUTION

Heneghan v Manchester Dry Docks Ltd & Others [2016] EWCA Civ 86

The case of *Heneghan* considered the circumstances of a claimant who had died from lung cancer (not mesothelioma) having been exposed to asbestos fibres, dust, and cigarette smoke. The defendants had employed him for a period totaling 35% of his working life. The epidemiological evidence confirmed that the asbestos exposure had doubled the risk of his developing the cancer.

Jay J at first instance considered submissions that the exposure had materially contributed the disease (as per *Bonnington Castings*) as opposed to the risk of the disease (as per *Fairchild*). The defendant argued that in the case of lung cancer, causation needed to be proved in accordance with the 'but for' test rather than by means of material contribution. The judge recognised that he was bound in terms of the determination of causation by the case of *AB* but expressly disagreed with the contention that material contribution was only applicable to cases of divisible injury:

> "*In my view, the Court of Appeal came to the same conclusion, albeit for different reasons, in paragraph 150 of its Judgment in Ministry of Defence v AB and others [2010] EWCA Civ 1317. Mr Allan criticised that part of the reasoning of the Court of Appeal which predicated the application of the material contribution principle on divisible conditions. I tend to agree with his criticism, but the fact remains that the Court of Appeal refused to apply the material contribution limb of Lord Reid's*

> *test (as originally formulated in 1956) to cancer cases resulting from radiation exposure*"[99].

Applying *Fairchild*, Jay J made an award of 35% of the amount claimed was made based on the proportion of time over which the defendants had materially increased the risk.

The claimant appealed on the basis that the defendants had materially contributed to the disease and therefore were liable on a 100% basis. It was argued that the exposure to the asbestos could be characterised as a cumulative exposure with each source of the asbestos making a material contribution to the carcinogenic disease process.

Providing the lead judgment, Lord Dyson made the following summary of the relevant principles of causation:

> "*There are three ways of establishing causation in disease cases. The first is by showing that but for the defendant's negligence, the claimant would not have suffered the disease. Secondly, where the disease is caused by the cumulative effect of an agency part of which is attributable to breach of duty on the part of the defendant and part of which involves no breach of duty, the defendant will be liable on the ground that his breach of duty made a 'material contribution' to the disease: Bonnington Castings Ltd v Wardlaw [1956] AC 613. The disease in that case was pneumoconiosis, which is a divisible disease (i.e. one whose severity increases with increased exposure to the agency). Thirdly, where causation cannot be proved in either of these ways, for example because the disease is indivisible, causation may be established if it is proved that the defendant materially*

---

99 *Heneghan v Manchester Dry Docks Ltd & Others [2014] EWHC 4190 (QB) [65]*

> *increased the risk of the victim contracting the disease: the Fairchild exception. Mesothelioma is an indivisible disease.*"[100]

Lord Dyson considered that the evidence did not allow the court to determine that exposure to the causative agent by any particular defendant had caused the disease. It was accepted that the defendants had increased the risk. Dismissing the claimant's appeal Lord Dyson concluded:

> "*The response of the law to the problem posed in a case where the scientific evidence does not permit a finding that the exposure attributable to a particular defendant contributed to the injury is to apply the Fairchild exception. The factors identified in Fairchild for the application of this solution exist in the present case: (i) all the defendants concede their breach of duty; (ii) all increased the risk that the deceased would contract lung cancer; (iii) all exposed the deceased to the same agency that was implicated in causation (asbestos fibres); but (iv) medical science is unable to determine to which (if any) of the defendants there should be attributed the exposure which actually caused the cell changes which initiated the genetic changes culminating in the cancer*"[101]

<u>AB v Ministry of Defence [2010] EWCA Civ. 1317</u>

This was a case before the Court of Appeal brought by a number of claimants who were employed by the defendant between 1952 and 1958 and who were involved in a series of atmospheric tests of thermonuclear devices in the Pacific Ocean. The allegations were that the defendant negligently exposed them to radiation which caused them to suffer various injuries including types of cancer. Limitation was heard as a preliminary issue. The defendant denied the claims and sought to have

[100] *Heneghan v Manchester Dry Docks Ltd & Others [2016] EWCA Civ 86 [23]*

[101] Ibid [47]

them struck out. Foskett J found that ten individual lead cases could proceed. The defendant appealed.

Smith LJ gave the lead judgment on appeal. The issues before the court included consideration of causation insofar as it related to the prospects of the cases. It was accepted that exposure to radiation was capable of causing types of cancers, although the risk was understood to be related to higher levels of exposure. None of the claimant's cases were assisted by medical evidence.

The starting point for the court was in identifying that the alleged conditions had several different potential causes including the alleged exposure to radiation. The burden was upon the claimant to prove on the balance of probabilities that radiation was causative. The defendant referred to the ruling of the House of Lords in *Wilsher*[102]. The defendant recognised the notion of doubling the risk was a recognised potential means of obtaining proof but argued that was not the case.

The defendant submitted that *Bonnington Castings* was inapplicable as the radiation exposure could not be said to have contributed to their conditions, only to the risk that they would occur. In responding to this Smith LJ stated in relation to *Bonnington Castings*:

> *"This type of modification of the 'but for' rule is still available where the negligent and non-negligent causative components have both contributed to the disease (as opposed to the risk of the disease) and it is not possible to apportion the harm caused and therefore the damages. This method of proving causation (by showing that the tort made a material contribution to the condition or disease) is only available where the severity of the disease is related to the amount of exposure; further exposure to the noxious substance in question is capable of making the condition worse. Thus, the MOD's submission is that, in the*

102 *Wilsher v Essex Area Health Authority [1988] 2 W.L.R. 557*

> *present cases, at least so far as the cancers were concerned, that could not be said. The cancers either developed or they did not. Their severity did not depend on the extent of the exposure. It could not be said that the exposure to radiation had made a material contribution to the disease, only to the risk that it might occur"*[103]

Smith LJ went on to confirm that the principle in *Bonnington Castings* "*applies only where the disease or condition is 'divisible' so that an increased dose of the harmful agent worsens the disease*"[104]. The judge also considered that in *Bailey* the injury to the claimant was a divisible dose related injury:

> "In *those cases, the pneumoconiosis and the weakness were divisible conditions. Cancer is an indivisible condition; one either gets it or one does not. The condition is not worse because one has been exposed to a greater or smaller amount of the causative agent"*[105]

In submissions, the claimants considered that with additional evidence, it may be possible to demonstrate that the radiation had made a material contribution to their conditions, hoping to apply *Bailey*. Alternatively, it was submitted that the exposure to radiation had materially increased the risk of developing cancer. It was recognised that this would require an extension of the narrow application of the material increase in risk test as set out in *Fairchild*.

The Court of Appeal dismissed the claims. The claimants appealed to the Supreme Court on the interpretation of the term "*knowledge*" within the Limitation Act 1980. Arguments regarding causation were not considered. The claims were dismissed.

---

[103] *AB v Ministry of Defence [2010] EWCA Civ. 1317 [134]*

[104] Ibid [150]

[105] *AB v Ministry of Defence [2010] EWCA Civ. 1317[150]*

Chapter Summary

i. In *Heneghan* and *AB* the Court of Appeal was asked to consider the applicability of the test for material contribution and that of material contribution to risk.

ii. In both cases the Court of Appeal confirmed the distinction between the two tests and had no appetite for extending the exception created in *Fairchild*.

iii. The Court of Appeal confirmed that the test for material contribution was limited in its application to cases where the disease or injury was divisible and dose related.

PART TWO

CLINICAL NEGLIGENCE

By the time material contribution was applied to clinical negligence cases, the key legal principles had been considered and developed in relation to occupational diseases stemming from *Bonnington Castings*. The case law in occupational disease related to single identifiable causative agents acting concurrently or consecutively from different sources.

In applying material contribution causation to clinical negligence cases, the courts would be asked to consider the causative potency of multiple potential causative agents. Where in clinical negligence cases multiple causative agents are in play, it is conceptually more difficult to argue that any one of them is more likely than another to materially increase the risk of injury. There has been no extension of the *Fairchild* exception in cases of clinical negligence. Policy considerations that applied to cases in which the relationship was employee and employer were not considered relevant.

CHAPTER SIX

UNSUCCESSFUL APPLICATION OF MATERIAL CONTRIBUTION IN CLINICAL NEGLIGENCE

Material contribution causation in the context of clinical negligence was first successful in the Court of Appeal case of *Bailey*[106]. Prior to that came the cases of *Hotson*[107] and *Wilsher*[108] which were unsuccessfully appealed to the House of Lords. In both of these cases, the courts were invited to infer causation in the face of multiple negligent and non-negligent causative agents.

Hotson v East Berkshire Area Health Authority [1987] 3WLR 232

The facts of this case involved a non-negligent fall from a tree and an alleged delay in treating the associated fracture. The claimant, aged 13 at the time of his injury, was assessed at the defendant's hospital whereby a fracture to his left femoral epiphysis went undiagnosed for a period of 5 days. The claimant sought damages to compensate for avascular necrosis to his epiphysis. This was associated with disability and the likelihood of developing osteoarthritis.

The defendant admitted breach of duty in failing to recognise and treat the claimant's injury promptly. At first instance, it was accepted that there was a 75% chance that avascular necrosis would have occurred on account of the non-negligent fall. The percentage probability was predicated on the notion that the cause of the avascular necrosis was

[106] *Bailey v Ministry of Defence [2008] EWCA Civ 883.*

[107] *Hotson v East Berkshire Area Health Authority [1987] 3WLR 232*

[108] *Wilsher v Essex Area Health Authority [1988] 2 W.L.R. 557*

either non-negligent damage to the epiphyseal blood vessels incurred at the time of the fall (75% chance) or negligent damage caused by subsequent bleeding, that absent the negligence could have been arrested (25% chance). The medical evidence could not devise which of these agents was the likely cause.

The trial judge awarded the claimant damages for the loss of the 25% chance that he would have made a full recovery. It remained the Defendant's case throughout that the 25% chance fell short of the 51% standard of proof that the claimant required to make his case on the balance of probabilities. The Court of Appeal dismissed the appeal by the health authority who went on to obtain permission to appeal to the House of Lords. The House of Lords allowed the defendant's appeal.

The claimant's primary case was argued based on a loss of chance. This was an invitation to disapply ordinary principles of causation and instead prefer statistical likelihood. The judgment of Lord Bridge did not consider that this was the type of clinical negligence case that was reliant upon the analysis of statistical probabilities:

> "*The plaintiff's evidence, at its highest, was that the delay in treatment was a material contributory cause. This was a conflict, like any other about some relevant past event, which the judge could not avoid resolving on a balance of probabilities. Unless the plaintiff proved on a balance of probabilities that the delayed treatment was at least a material contributory cause of the avascular necrosis he failed on the issue of causation and no question of quantification could arise*"[109].

Lord Bridge confirmed that that to make out causation, the standard of proof for material contribution was the balance of probabilities. Under the circumstances that the failure to diagnose and treat the avascular necrosis had been demonstrated to have materially contributed to the

[109] *Hotson v East Berkshire Area Health Authority [1987] 3WLR 232* [782]

development of avascular necrosis, the claimant would have succeeded in recovering damages on 100% basis:

> "*I know of no principle of English law which would have entitled the authority to a discount from the full measure of damage to reflect the chance that, even given prompt treatment, avascular necrosis might well still have developed*"[110].

<u>Wilsher v Essex Area Health Authority [1988] 2 W.L.R. 557</u>

The claimant was a premature baby being nursed in a special care baby unit at the defendant hospital. Supplementary oxygen was required. To accurately monitor the levels of oxygen, cannulation of the umbilical artery was attempted. The clinician negligently cannulated the umbilical vein with the result that the levels of oxygen recorded were lower. Oxygen was then administered based on the lower readings.

The claimant developed retrolental fibrodysplasia (RLF), a condition of the eyes that resulted in blindness. The claimant sought damages in respect of the negligent treatment in the special care baby unit. It was established through evidence that there were several agents that had the potential to have caused the RLF. One of these was negligent administration of excess oxygen. The claimant alleged that excessive levels of oxygen negligently occurred on several occasions. The other potentially non-negligent causative agents were apnea, hypercarbia, intraventricular hemorrhage, patent ductus arteriosus, all of which the claimant had experienced prior to being diagnosed with RLF.

The trial lasted 20 days. The expert evidence as to the cause of the RLF was described as "*voluminous*" and "*irreconcilable*"[111]. The court at first instance found the defendant liable on the basis that there was a burden upon the defendant to prove that the claimant's condition had not been

---

[110] Ibid [783]

[111] *Wilsher v Essex Area Health Authority [1988] 2 W.L.R. 557* [1081]

caused by the clinicians. The case was appealed. Lord Mustill applied *McGhee* to conclude that where "*one party owes a duty not to conduct himself in that way; and if the first party does conduct himself in that way; and if the other party does suffer injury of the kind to which the risk related; then the first party is taken to have caused the injury by his breach of duty, even though the existence and extent of the contribution made by the breach cannot be ascertained*"[112]. The Court of Appeal dismissed the defendant's appeal. The case was appealed to the House of Lords.

It was argued on the part of the claimant that following *Bonnington Castings* "*the question for determination in a case like the present is that the plaintiff only has to show that there was a material contribution to the cause of his injury*"[113]. In terms of causation, it was argued by the claimant that the prematurity made the retinal blood vessels affected by the RLF vulnerable to assault from inter alia the excessive treatment with oxygen. The defendant did not accept that the levels of oxygen that the claimant was subjected to materially increased the injury or the risk of developing RLF.

Lord Bridge framed the causative potency of the administration of oxygen as one of number of possible causes of RLF. It was clarified that (perhaps contrary to the opinion of Lord Wilberforce in *McGhee*) the burden of proof in all respects including causation rested with the claimant "*McGhee v. National Coal Board [1973] 1 W.L.R. 1 laid down no new principle of law whatever. On the contrary, it affirmed the principle that the onus of proving causation lies on the pursuer or plaintiff*"[114].

Lord Bridge distinguished *Bonnington Castings* and *McGhee* on the basis that in both of those cases there was only one agent that was certain to have caused the injury. Both occupational disease cases concerned the potential contribution between the negligent and non-negligent versions

112 *McGhee v National Coal Board [1973] 1 WLR 1 [771-772]*

113 *Wilsher v Essex Area Health Authority [1988] 2 W.L.R. 557 [1078]*

114 *Wilsher v Essex Area Health Authority [1988] 2 W.L.R. 557* [1090]

of that agent. Lord Bridge quoted and affirmed the dissenting view of Sir Nicholas Browne Wilkinson in the court below:

> "*In the present case the question is different. There are a number of different agents which could have caused the RLF. Excess oxygen was one of them. The defendants failed to take reasonable precautions to prevent one of the possible causative agents (e.g., excess oxygen) from causing RLF. But no one can tell in this case whether excess oxygen did or did not cause or contribute to the RLF suffered by the plaintiff.*
>
> *The position, to my mind, is wholly different from that in the McGhee [1973] 1 W.L.R. 1, case where there was only one candidate (brick dust) which could have caused the dermatitis, and the failure to take a precaution against brick dust causing dermatitis was followed by dermatitis caused by brick dust. In such a case, I can see the common sense, if not the logic, of holding that, in the absence of any other evidence, the failure to take the precaution caused or contributed to the dermatitis. To the extent that certain members of the House of Lords decided the question on inferences from evidence or presumptions, I do not consider that the present case falls within their reasoning. A failure to take preventative measures against one out of five possible causes is no evidence as to which of those five caused the injury.*"[115]

The House of Lords decided against allowing material contribution to rescue the claimant. Arguably, it was the inadequacies of medical science that prevented the claimant from proving which agent likely caused or contributed to his injury. In the absence of that knowledge, the causative potency of the negligent agent could not be proven on the balance of probabilities. The defendant's appeal was allowed.

---

[115] Ibid [1091]

Gregg v Scott No. [2005] UKHL 2

The case of *Gregg* deserves a mention. The defendant's negligent 9-month delay in his diagnosis of cancer reduced his statistical chances of recovery from 45% at the time of the negligence to 25% at the time of trial. Inglis J at first instance applied the reasoning set out in Hotson. The Court of Appeal by a majority dismissed the claimant's appeal.

As with *Hotson*, the claimant did not plead their case in material contribution nor as a "*lost years*" claim. Instead, the claimant sought to recover on the basis that they had been deprived of the loss of a greater chance of recovery. The House of Lords by a majority dismissed the claimant's claim.

The judgment of the House of Lords contained some analysis of the quantification of losses and the use of statistics in clinical negligence claims. The fundamental issue for the claimant was the failure to discharge the burden upon them that the negligence had on the balance of probabilities caused an actionable loss. Lord Hoffmann amongst the majority who found against the claimant made the following observations:

> *"Everything has a determinate cause, even if we do not know what it is. The blood-starved hip joint in Hotson's case, the blindness in Wilsher 's case, the mesothelioma in Fairchild 's case; each had its cause and it was for the plaintiff to prove that it was an act or omission for which the defendant was responsible. The narrow terms of the exception made to this principle in Fairchild's case only serves to emphasise the strength of the rule.*
>
> *The fact that proof is rendered difficult or impossible because no examination was made at the time, as in Hotson's case, or because medical science cannot provide the answer, as in Wilsher's case, makes no difference. There is no inherent uncertainty about what caused something to happen in the past*

> *or about whether something which happened in the past will cause something to happen in the future. Everything is determined by causality. What we lack is knowledge and the law deals with lack of knowledge by the concept of the burden of proof."*[116]

Chapter Summary

i. The cases of *Hotson and Wilsher* illustrated the preliminary requirement for the claimant to prove on the balance of probabilities that the loss was caused by the negligence complained of.

ii. Where multiple causative agents are in play and their precise causative potency cannot be determined, a claimant cannot rely upon inferences drawn by the court to bridge the evidential gap. This was commented upon by Lord Toulson in case of *Williams*:

> *"A claim will fail if the most that can be said is that the claimant's injury is likely to have been caused by one or more of a number of disparate factors, one of which was attributable to a wrongful act or omission of the defendant. In such a case the claimant will not have shown as a matter of probability that the factor attributable to the defendant caused the injury or was one of two or more factors which operated cumulatively to cause it…the fact that the administration of excess oxygen was negligent did not warrant an inference that it was a more likely cause of the RLF than the various other known possible causes."*

iii. The injuries in *Hotson* nor *Wilsher* were expressly considered in terms of their divisibility. Retrospectively applying these notions, it seems likely that the overall injuries in both cases were

[116] Gregg v Scott No. [2005] UKHL 2 [79]

indivisible. The negligent processes in *Hotson* (reduction in epiphyseal blood supply) may have been divisible but it was considered unlikely that the negligent version of this agent was on the balance of probabilities the causative agent. The apportionment applied by the lower courts in *Hotson* may only have been reasonable if divisibility of a cumulative process had been established.

CHAPTER SEVEN

SUCCESSFUL APPLICATION OF MATERIAL CONTRIBUTION IN CLINICAL NEGLIGENCE

Bailey v Ministry of Defence [2008] EWCA Civ 883

Bailey represented a watershed moment in the application of material contribution in clinical negligence. The claimant successfully argued that breach of duty had materially contributed to their losses. The applicability of material contribution to the facts has been subsequently scrutinized. Courts and academics have considered the extent to which concepts of divisibility and indivisibility can be applied to the process by which Ms Bailey's injury occurred and to her injury.

On 9 January 2001, the claimant was admitted to the defendant hospital for surgery to treat a gallstone. The procedure (ERCP) took place on 11 January 2001. During the procedure bleeding was noted. During the post operative period of 11-12 January 2001, the claimant became unwell and developed pancreatitis. The pancreatitis itself was a recognised and non-negligent complication of the procedure. The claimant alleged however that the defendant failed to adequately resuscitate her over a period of approximately 20 hours post-operatively ("the period of negligent care").

On the afternoon of 12 January 2001, Ms Bailey was transferred to a high dependency unit. She continued to deteriorate and on 14 January 2001, was transferred to an Intensive care department (ITU) where she underwent a gastroscopy. On 15 January 2001, she underwent a further investigative procedure (PCT). Following this she was taken to theatre to manage bleeding caused by the PCT and to perform a cholecystectomy. She returned to theatre on 19 January 2001 to have surgical packs removed. The claimant was noted to have ongoing renal failure, pancreatitis, and sepsis.

On 26 January 2001, her clinical condition stabilised. The claimant was transferred to the renal ward at another hospital. That evening she was given approximately 100mls of lemonade to drink which she immediately aspirated into her lungs. This led to a cardiac arrest and subsequent brain damage.

The claimant argued that absent the period of negligent care, she would not have had to undergo all of her subsequent surgery, and although she would likely still have suffered pancreatitis and renal failure, her clinical condition would have been improved. The alleged reason for the claimant being unable to prevent the aspiration was her extreme weakness because of her lengthy illness which had been materially contributed to by the period of negligence.

The claimant urged the court to apply the test for material contribution citing *Hotson, Wilsher, Fairchild, and Gregg*. The defendant sought to distinguish between the concepts of material increase in risk and material contribution of injury. Placing reliance on *Wilsher*, the defendant submitted that material contribution was not applicable where the claimant was unable to prove on the balance of probabilities that the injury was caused by the alleged negligent agent.

At first instance, Foskett J accepted that the cardiac arrest had been caused by the Ms Bailey's "*weakness*" which was formed of two "components", the weakness caused by the pancreatitis and that caused by the defendant's negligent lack of care over the period of negligent care. Foskett J also found as a fact that absent the negligence, a further procedure would likely have taken place on 12 January 2001. The negligent period of care was thereby found to have materially contributed to the overall weakness:

> "*I am satisfied, on the balance of probabilities, that she had not and that she was weakened as a result. I cannot say whether the*

contribution made by this component was more or less than that made by the pancreatitis, and it follows that I cannot say whether the contribution made by the pancreatitis was greater or smaller than the contribution of the other component. All I can say is that the natural inference is that each contributed materially to the overall weakness, and it was the overall weakness that caused the aspiration."[117]

The mechanism by which the weakness caused the aspiration was characterised as:

> "*a commonsense assumption ... that the claimant's generally weakened and debilitated condition on 26 January caused her not to be able to respond naturally and effectively to the emergence of vomit ... that she inhaled it.*"[118].

Of note, no specific mention was made of the need to apply a modified version of the 'but for' test. The defendant appealed.

Giving the lead judgment, Waller LJ considered that the inability to perform further surgery on 12 January 2001, was a consequence of the claimant's weakened and unresuscitated state. Similarly, it was open to the trial judge to find that it was the claimant's weakened state that led to her aspirating "*if she had been able to respond naturally, she would have done so*"[119]

Waller LJ agreed with the trial judge that the causative agent was the weakness, quoting Foskett' s judgment at paragraph 60:

> "*Even leaving out of account the independent effect of the pancreatitis, it defies all common sense to say that she had*

[117] Bailey v MOD [2007] EWHC 2913 (QB) [60]

[118] Ibid [54]

[119] Bailey v Ministry of Defence [2008] EWCA Civ 883 [32]

> *recovered from the effects of all that by 26 January. I am satisfied, on the balance of probabilities, that she had not and that she was weakened as a result. I cannot say whether the contribution made by this component was more or less than that made by the pancreatitis, and it follows that I cannot say whether the contribution made by the pancreatitis was greater or smaller than the contribution of the other component. All I can say is that the natural inference is that each contributed materially to the overall weakness and it was the overall weakness that caused the aspiration".*

Waller LJ distinguished *Wilshire* on the basis that that was a case involved "*different distinct causes which operated in a different way and might have caused the injury and where the claimant could not establish which cause either "caused or contributed" to his injury*"[120]. Similarly, *Hotson* was distinguished on the basis that the evidence in that case suggested that the injury would likely have occurred in any event.

The Court of Appeal dismissed the appeal, summarising their reasons for departing from standard causative principles as follows:

> "*...ordinarily in a case of medical negligence resulting in injury it was for a claimant to prove on a balance of probabilities that but for the negligence the injury would not have occurred; that in a case involving cumulative causes, where medical science could not establish the probability that but for a particular act of negligence the injury would not have occurred, but could establish that the contribution of the negligent cause was material or something more than negligible, the court was entitled to apply a modified test; that, consequently, it was sufficient for the claimant to establish on a balance of probabilities that the first defendants' lack of care had made a material contribution to the weakness of her condition which led*

[120] Bailey v Ministry of Defence [2008] EWCA Civ 883 [44]

> *to her cardiac arrest and hypoxic brain damage; and that, accordingly, the judge had applied the correct test and had been entitled to conclude that the first defendants were liable for the claimant's brain damage*"[121]

Waller LJ concluded by setting out his analysis of "*cumulative cause cases*"[122]. The relevant points can be summarised as follows:

i. There was no distinction between clinical negligence cases and other types of case.

ii. Where the evidence demonstrates on the balance of probabilities that the injury would have occurred in non-tortious circumstances, the claim will fail as per *Hotson.*

iii. If the injury would not have occurred 'but for' the negligence, the claim succeeds.

iv. Where gaps in medical science stand in the way of establishing 'but for' causation but where the contribution of a negligent agent can be proven (on the balance of probabilities) to be more than negligible, the material contribution test can be applied, and the claim succeeds.

Subsequent analysis of Bailey

Was the injury in Bailey divisible or indivisible? Certainly, the process by which the injury occurred (the weakness) on the analysis of Foskett J appeared to be divisible into two constituent components which were described as cumulative. The overall injury itself, however, for which the claimant sought to recover (the brain damage) was indivisible.

---

[121] Ibid [46]

[122] Ibid [46]

In *AB* Smith LJ sought to distinguish the position of the claimants in AB with reference to Bailey"... *we accept that, at least so far as cancers are concerned, the claimants cannot rely on proving that the radiation exposure has made a material contribution to the disease, as in Bailey and Bonnington Castings...the tort did not increase the risk of harm; it increased the actual harm. Similarly in Bailey, the tort (a failure of medical care) increased the claimant's physical weakness. She would have been quite weak in any event as the result of a condition she had developed naturally. No one could say how great a contribution each had made to the overall weakness save that each was material. It was the overall weakness which led to the claimant's failure to protect her airway when she vomited with the result that she inhaled her vomit and suffered a cardiac arrest and brain damage"*[123]

Smith LJ considered that the weakness in *Bailey* was the divisible injury. As explained in the above passage, she considered the relative contribution made by negligent and non-negligent components to be impossible to separate. It may be argued that because "*No one could say how great a contribution each had made to the overall weakness" (as above)* the injury in Bailey may reasonably be described as indivisible.

In *the case of Williams* the Privy Council analysed the causation case in *Bailey*. In obiter, the court opined that based on the facts of the case, the judge at first instance was right to hold the hospital responsible in law for the consequences of the aspiration. The Privy Council considered however that this finding could have been reached on standard 'but for' causative principles without the need to apply material contribution:

> " *As to the parallel weakness of the claimant due to her pancreatitis, the case may be seen as an example of the well-known principle that a tortfeasor takes his victim as he finds her. The Board does not share the view of the Court of Appeal that the case involved a departure from the "but-for" test. The judge concluded that the totality of the claimant's weakened condition*

[123] *AB v Ministry of Defence [2010] EWCA Civ. 1317[150]*

> *caused the harm. If so, "but-for" causation was established. The fact that her vulnerability was heightened by her pancreatitis no more assisted the hospital's case than if she had an eggshell skull"*[124]

Miss Melissa Rich (A Protected Party by Her Mother and Litigation Friend Helen Rich) v Hull and East Yorkshire Hospitals NHS Trust [2015] EWHC 3395

The case of *Rich* concerned the alleged failure to administer corticosteroid medication prior to delivery of the claimant by c-section. The claimant alleged that the failure had caused or materially contributed to her developing post-natal Respiratory Distress Syndrome (RDS) requiring mechanical ventilation and resulting in Periventricular Leukomalacia (PVL) and cerebral palsy.

The claimant relied upon the findings in Bailey. Jay J approved the findings of Foskett J at first instance and described the injury as indivisible "*Given that Hotson was inapplicable because it could not be established on the balance of probabilities that the cardiac arrest would not have occurred without the negligent causes, it was sufficient for the Claimant's purposes that the negligence had contributed to the indivisible outcome*"[125]

In relation to the findings of the Court of Appeal in *Bailey*, Jay J referred to academic criticism of the judgment:

> "*contention is that it is unnecessary to require any modification of the "but for" test at all; it is sufficient in this type of case for the Claimant to prove that the Defendant's negligence contributed to the mechanism which led to her indivisible injury. This is the principle which may be derived from logic*

[124] *Williams v The Bermuda Hospitals Board [2016] UKPC* [47]

[125] Miss Melissa Rich (A Protected Party by Her Mother and Litigation Friend Helen Rich) v Hull and East Yorkshire Hospitals NHS Trust [2015] EWHC 3395 [200]

> *and jurisprudence. I agree...that the characterisation of the negligent mechanism of injury in Bailey as being one of several cumulative causes is uncomfortable, given that the analogy of silica dust (with each grain of dust causing a separate physical insult) appears incomplete. The "cumulative cause" analysis works much better in a case of divisible injury"*[126].

Jay J concluded that the injury in *Bailey* was the combined cardiac arrest and brain damage, and that this injury was indivisible. He considered that a plausible mechanism of causation would have been to find that the negligence made a material contribution to the mechanism that caused this indivisible injury "*it would be much neater...to say that the Defendant's tort contributed to the mechanism which led to Ms Bailey's indivisible injury or injuries*"[127]. As it was, the judgment of Waller J characterised the injury as being the weakened state to which the negligence made a cumulative contribution. This was the process that in *AB* Smith LJ characterised as divisible.

In *Rich,* Mr Jay J dismissed the claimant's case on breach. In his analysis of causation, he concluded that he was bound by the ratio in Bailey and made the following findings:

i. The RDS and PVL were indivisible injuries.

ii. Administration of corticosteroids would have made the injuries less severe.

iii. The failure to give corticosteroids materially contributed to the injury rather than materially contributing to the risk of the injury.

---

[126] Ibid [202-203]

[127] Ibid [205]

iv. Medical science was unable to assist in determining what would have happened on the balance of probabilities but for the defendant's tort.

v. Applying Bailey, the defendant's tort materially contributed to the claimant's damage. The claimant would have recovered in full had breach of duty been determined.

Williams v The Bermuda Hospitals Board [2016] UKPC [32]

When the case was heard at first instance, the judge found the defendant negligent in terms of delay but that the claimant's case in causation failed. This decision on causation was overturned by the Court of Appeal before being appealed by the defendant. The Privy Council committee consisted of Lady Hale, Lord Clarke, Lord Hughes, Lord Toulson and Lord Hodge. Their findings are not binding but their analysis of material contribution is unignorable.

On 30 May 2011 at around 11.17 am, the claimant presented to A&E at the defendant hospital complaining of abdominal pain. A diagnosis of acute appendicitis was considered. At around 13.10, to confirm the diagnosis, a CT scan was ordered. The CT was not requested as an emergency and was performed at 17.27. A report of the CT scan was received at around 19.30. The findings of the report were then discussed with a surgeon. Mr Williams was taken to theatre at around 21.30.

The trial judge considered that on account of the failure to order the CT as an emergency, there were delays surrounding the provision of the CT and its reporting. A counterfactual timeline was adopted by which in the absence of negligent delay, the operation should have taken place between 17.15 and 19.10. This reflected a delay in performing the operation of between four hours and 15 minutes and two hours and 20 minutes.

At surgery, the appendix was found to have ruptured causing pus and phlegmon to be present throughout the abdominal cavity. Following expert evidence, the trial judge characterised the rupture of the appendix as a gradual process that had likely begun around 15.19.

The extension of sepsis was considered to have affected the adequacy of the blood supply to the claimant's heart causing a myocardial ischemic event. It was accepted that the extent of the infection would have been reduced had surgery taken place earlier. During the operation, the claimant's blood pressure dropped. Following surgery, the claimant required treatment in intensive care (ITU).

The trial judge found as a fact that the sepsis from the ruptured appendix had caused injury to the claimant's heart and lungs. In terms of his findings on causation, he found the claimant to have failed to prove that the complications that he developed during and after surgery were probably caused by the defendant's failure to diagnose and treat him expeditiously. Had the CT scan been obtained and interpreted promptly these complications might have been avoided but was not satisfied that they probably would have been avoided. The appendix had ruptured, and sepsis had begun during the non-negligent period prior to surgery, regardless of any negligence. An award was made reflecting 2 hours of avoidable pain and suffering.

The Bermudan Court of Appeal confirmed various negligent delays but overturned the judge's finding on causation. Applying the modification to the 'but for' test as set out in Bailey, the appellant court found for the claimant on the basis that the delays had material contributed to the claimant's injury.

Before the Judicial Committee of the Privy Council, the defendant contested the applicability of material contribution seeking to distinguish *Bonnington Castings*, as in that case:

i. There was a single causative agent.

ii. The tortious contribution was more than minimal.

iii. The contribution of the tortious agent was concurrent with the non-tortious agent.

iv. The tortious contribution increased the magnitude of the harm (as opposed to simply the risk).

The judgment of the Privy Council was delivered by Lord Toulson. The relevance of *Bonnington Castings* was considered. The process which caused the injury to Mr Williams was confirmed by the Privy Council as sepsis. Following analysis by the Privy Council, the counterfactual timeline was found to be slightly inaccurate. The sepsis had been found to have likely begun around 15.19. In the absence of negligence, it was found that surgery should have taken place between 17.15 and 18.10 (a minimum of two hours and 20 minutes earlier than it in fact did). At that point, the process of sepsis had begun. At the time of the operation, the sepsis had developed over 6 hours.

As a starting point Lord Toulson began with an academic observation:

> *"As Professor Sarah Green has succinctly observed (Causation in Negligence, Hart Publishing, 2015, Chapter 5, p 97):*
>
> *It is trite negligence law that, where possible, defendants should only be held liable for that part of the claimant's ultimate damage to which they can be causally linked ... It is equally trite that, where a defendant has been found to have caused or contributed to an indivisible injury, she will be held fully liable for it, even though there may well have been other contributing causes ..."*[128].

The concept of divisibility or indivisibility of the injury was not one that was expressly explored in the House of Lords judgment in Bonnington Castings. Nevertheless, Lord Toulson considered that pneumoconiosis

[128] Williams v The Bermuda Hospitals Board [2016] UKPC [31]

was not characterised by the Court of Appeal as a disease that was dose dependent. Lord Toulson noted that:

> "*Lord Reid interpreted the medical evidence as meaning that the particles from the swing grinders were a cause of the entire disease. True, they were only part of the cause, but they were a partial cause of the entire injury, as distinct from being a cause of only part of the injury*"[129]

On the basis that the pneumoconiosis was indivisible, it was not therefore necessary for the claimant to prove that the negligent causative agent (the "guilty dust") was responsible for the actual injury suffered. All the claimant needed to prove was that the guilty dust had contributed more than minimally to the cumulative injury.

The Privy Council rejected the notion that *Bonnington Castings* was distinguishable on the basis that the tortious and non-tortious agents had to be operating concurrently. The circumstances in *Williams* were described as a case of a single known agent, sepsis from the ruptured appendix. The Privy Council concluded:

> "*The sepsis was not divided into separate components causing separate damage to the heart and lungs. Its development and effect on the heart and lungs was a single continuous process, during which the sufficiency of the supply of oxygen to the heart steadily reduced*"[130]

The judgments in *Hotson*, *McGhee*, and *Wilsher* were reviewed. In terms of sequence in which the causative agents operated, the court referred to the judgment in *McGhee* which considered it immaterial whether they do so concurrently or successively. *Wilsher* was distinguished on the basis

[129] Williams v The Bermuda Hospitals Board [2016] UKPC [32]

[130] Williams v The Bermuda Hospitals Board [2016] UKPC [41]

that the potential causative agents were "*disparate*", rather than all forming part of an identifiable and cumulative process.

Dr Sido John v Central Manchester and Manchester Children's University Hospitals NHS Foundation Trust [2016] EWHC 407 (QB)

The case of *John* was heard in the High Court before Picken J. The judgment of the Privy Council in *Williams* had been handed down the week before the start of the trial.

The claimant was a GP. He had suffered an intra-cranial infection at age 16 that had left him with a mild right sided hemiparesis. In the early hours of 23 December 2007, he fell whilst climbing stairs at his home, sustaining a head injury. He was found two hours later and was taken to the defendant A&E. He was admitted at around 06.52. A CT scan of his head was planned but was not performed until 13.12. In the meantime, the claimant was transferred to the clinical decisions unit of A&E. His reported Glasgow Coma Score (GCS) indicating his level of consciousness, remained reduced, and he was noted to have word finding difficulties (expressive dysphasia). The CT scan demonstrated him to have an acute sub-dural hematoma (a collection of blood in the subdural space around his brain). The claimant had a seizure following which he was intubated and ventilated. Following this there was a delay of approximately one hour in arranging transfer for him to another hospital for definitive surgery. He eventually had a left fronto-parietal craniotomy and excavation of the hematoma at about 19.30.

The claimant alleged that there were negligent delays both in the arranging of the CT scan and the ambulance transfer. It was the claimant's case that the raised intra-cranial pressure over the periods of the negligent delay had materially contributed to his overall brain injury.

The defendant contended that there were other non-negligent agents operating. The head injury itself was caused by the non-negligent fall and it was this that had led to the raised intra-cranial pressure. Furthermore, following the operation, the claimant developed a non-negligent intra-cranial infection which led to him being returned to theatre to undergo further surgery. The claimant was left with a cognitive and neuropsychological injury. It was considered unlikely that he would return to his role as a GP again.

The defendant initially argued that causation needed to be established applying standard 'but for' principles. In the alternative, the defendant proposed the appropriate question to ask was "*whether, if there was damaging raised intra-cranial pressure caused by negligence on the part of the Defendant, that raised intra-cranial pressure made a 'material contribution' to the damage which Dr John has suffered*"[131]. The defendant argued that damages should be apportioned according to the tortious and non-tortious elements of the injury.

In determining causation, the judge was directed to consider the case law including *Bonnington Castings*, *Bailey* and *Williams*. It was confirmed that the application of material contribution as set out in *Bonnington Castings* was not confined to cases of breach of statutory duty in occupational disease cases but was of "*general application*"[132].

The defendant initially sought to characterise the case as one with multiple discrete potentially causative agents (the initial head injury, a period of non-negligent raised intracranial pressure, and the intra-cranial infection) that was thereby analogous to *Wilsher* and distinguishable from *Bonnington, Bailey and Williams* (referred to as "*single agency*" cases). The judge considered that this was not a true distinction and that the central issue in *Wilsher* was not that it was a multiple agency case but rather the claimant had failed to prove on the balance of probabilities that the negligent provision of excessive oxygen had contributed to the injury.

---

131 Dr Sido John v Central Manchester and Manchester Children's University Hospitals NHS Foundation Trust [2016] EWHC 407 (QB) [4]

132 Dr Sido John v Central Manchester and Manchester Children's University Hospitals NHS Foundation Trust [2016] EWHC 407 (QB) [84]

Picken J concluded "*In short, the 'material contribution' approach applies, in my view, just as much to multiple factor cases as it does to 'single agency' cases*"[133].

Having determined that material contribution could apply to the circumstances of the case, Picken J went on to assess whether negligence materially contributed to the injury:

i. The first evidential issue addressed by the judge was whether the claimant had raised intra-cranial pressure prior to undergoing surgery and if so, the magnitude of that pressure and its likely causative potency. The judge considered that the claimant's evolving clinical deterioration was a manifestation of raised intra-cranial pressure for over the seven hours before he came to be operated upon. The Judge considered that the claimant had approximately six hours of avoidable raised intra-cranial pressure.

ii. The second issue was assessing whether on the balance of probabilities the raised intracranial pressure was causative to the claimant's injury. This was the stage in *Wilsher*[134] where the claimant's case failed because the experts were unable to form any consensus. The experts in John were broadly in agreement that if there was a period of damaging raised intra-cranial pressure then this would have likely made an unqualifiable yet more than *de minimis* contribution to the claimant's impairment. It was not possible to separate the relative contribution of the initial trauma, the extended period of raised intracranial pressure, and the post operative infection.

[133] Ibid [97]

[134] *Wilsher v Essex Area Health Authority [1988] 2 W.L.R. 557*

Having accepted in closing submissions to the applicability of material contribution in establishing causation, the defendant raised a second argument that the claimant should not be compensated for the totality of his injury. The court was asked to apply *Holtby*[135] to reduce and apportion damages to reflect the extent of the defendant's responsibility. Picken J considered the apportioning of damages where the evidence has not allowed for the attribution of damage to a specific cause. He considered the findings of Stuart-Smith LJ in *Holtby* citing from Mustill J in *Thompson*[136]:

> "*Thus, whatever the position might be if the court were to find itself unable to make any findings at all on the issue of causation and was accordingly being faced with a choice between awarding for the defendants in full, or for the plaintiffs in full, or on some wholly arbitrary basis such as an award of 50 per cent., I see no reason why the present impossibility of making a precise apportionment of impairment and disability in terms of time, should in justice lead to the result that the defendants are adjudged liable to pay in full, when it is known that only part of the damage was their fault. What justice does demand, to my mind, is that the court should make the best estimate which it can, in the light of the evidence, making the fullest allowances in favour of the plaintiffs for the uncertainties known to be involved in any apportionment. In the end, notwithstanding all the care lavished on it by the scientists and by counsel I believe that this has to be regarded as a jury question, and I propose to approach it as such.*"[137]

---

135 *Holtby v Brigham & Cowan (Hull) Ltd [2000 WL 345159]*

136 Dr Sido John v Central Manchester and Manchester Children's University Hospitals NHS Foundation Trust [2016] EWHC 407 (QB) [99]

137 Thompson v Smiths Shiprepairers (North Shields) Ltd [1984] ICR 236 [443G]

Picken J concluded that there were cases where it would be difficult to apportion damages and those where it would be impossible. He characterised that Bailey and Williams were cases where apportionment would have been impossible. Picken J rejected apportionment in the index case on the basis that it was "*impossible to attribute particular causes to particular loss*"[138]

Chapter Summary

i. *Bailey* was a watershed case in which material contribution causation was successfully applied. Bailey remains good law and is binding in applicable cases.

ii. The claimant's success in *Bailey* was on account of the manner in which the court characterised her deterioration. The weakness was identified as the relevant process which, on the balance of probabilities, caused the injury. The weakness itself was contributed to by both negligent and non-negligent agents. The precise role of the negligence could not be isolated due to lack of scientific understanding.

iii. Applying notions of divisibility and indivisibility, Smith LJ in *AB* referred to the injury in *Bailey* as divisible. Jay J in *Rich* characterised the cardiac arrest and brain injury and brain injury in *Bailey* as indivisible.

iv. *Williams* is authority for the proposition that material contribution applies where causative agents are operating consecutively. The injury in *Williams* was characterised by the Privy Council as indivisible. The process that led to the injury (the sepsis) was, however, a cumulative injury composed of

[138] Dr Sido John v Central Manchester and Manchester Children's University Hospitals NHS Foundation Trust [2016] EWHC 407 (QB) [100]

negligent and non-negligent periods of time. The process may reasonably be characterised as divisible.

v. The damage in *John* was the brain damage. On the facts of this case, there were multiple potential causative agents in play, all of which had the potential to cause brain damage. The judge found that the negligent delay that on the balance of probabilities led to a period of raised intracranial pressure that made a more than minimal contribution. Picken J confirmed that material contribution was a principle of "*general application*".

CHAPTER EIGHT

APPORTIONMENT

Apportionment in Occupational Disease cases

Holtby v Brigham & Cowan (Hull) Ltd [2000 WL 345159]

In *Holtby* the Court of Appeal considered the issue of apportionment in cases of material contribution where the disease was divisible:

> "*The question is this: where a claimant suffers injury, in this case asbestosis, as a result of exposure to a noxious substance by two or more persons, is the defendant who is one of those persons whose tortious act has made a material contribution to the injury, liable in respect of the whole resulting disability, subject only to such rights as he only has against other tortfeasors? Or, is he liable only to the extent that he has contributed toward the disability?*"[139]

The claimant worked as a maritime fitter. During his working life, he had been exposed to asbestos and had developed asbestosis. Asbestosis is a divisible dose related disease. For around half of this time he had been employed by the defendant. At first instance HHJ Altman considered the defendant liable for 75% of the damage. The claimant appealed on the basis that by correctly applying the principle of material contribution, no deduction should have been made.

The claimant relied upon *Bonnington Castings* to argue that material contribution did not allow for apportionment. It was accepted that in *Bonnington Castings* the matter of apportionment was not considered and acknowledged that in that case the claimant had suffered concurrent

139 *Holtby v Brigham & Cowan (Hull) Ltd [2000 WL 345159] [1]*

exposure to the causative agent. The claimant in *Holtby* argued that the same principle should apply to sequential causes.

Stuart- Smith LJ (quoting from Longmore J in the asbestosis case of *Milner v* Humphreys *and Glasgow Ltd [unreported]*) considered it material that the claimant was sequentially exposed to asbestos and the damage caused by this exposure was likely cumulative. Making the defendant liable for all the claimant's loss would thereby be unjust. The claimant's appeal was dismissed, Stuart-Smith LJ upholding the judge's apportionment:

> *"It might be said that the judge should have made the defendants liable only to 50 per cent. If the other employers had been before the court, then subject to exposure which ought to be considered de minimis, I think this is what he would have done. As it is he erred on the side of generosity to the claimant. No one criticises him for that. This method of dividing responsibility on a time exposure basis is, I understand, adopted among insurers in such cases as these. In the absence of some unusual feature, such as for example periods of exposure to a particularly dangerous blue asbestos during some periods, that seems to me to be not only the sensible, but correct approach in law. In practice, many years afterwards, such distinctions are likely to be impossible to prove."*[140]

The feature that distinguished *Holtby* from *Bonnington Castings* was not the nature of the disease but rather the defendant in *Holtby* seeking to apportion the injury based on its divisibility. Stuart-Smith LJ referred to the judgment of Mustill J in *Thompson:*

> *"As Mustill J. pointed out in Thompson at p441, the Bonnington principle is but a variant of the principle that, where an injury is indivisible, any tortfeasor whose act has been*

[140] Ibid [25]

a proximate case must compensate for the whole injury, leaving the tortfeasor to sort out with other possible tortfeasors any other appropriate claim for contribution, see Dingle v Associated Newspapers [1961] 2 QB 188 per Devlin LJ. Where there are causes concurrent in time, the likelihood is that a resulting injury will be indivisible; but where causes are sequential in time, it is not likely that an injury will be truly indivisible especially if the injury is a disease which can get worse with cumulative exposure"[141]. The progression of the asbestosis was found to be related to exposure. Apportionment was thereby achievable because asbestosis was divisible, and dose related.

Apportionment in Clinical Negligence cases

Setting aside the question of whether material contribution can be applied to indivisible injuries, the concept of divisibility is helpful in the apportioning of damages. Lord Toulson in *Sienkiewicz* stated:

> *"... Where the disease is indivisible, such as lung cancer, a defendant who has tortiously contributed to the cause of the disease will be liable in full. Where the disease is divisible, such as asbestosis, the tortfeasor will be liable in respect of the share of the disease for which he is responsible..."*[142].

In *John*[143], having found for the claimant in respect of his brain injury the court was invited to apportion the damages. In respect of both past loss of earnings and future loss of earnings, the court was asked to consider what the claimant's residual earnings capacity would have been 'but for' the non-negligent fall. In respect of past loss of earnings, the court accepted that there would have been some delay in the claimant

141 *Holtby v Brigham & Cowan (Hull) Ltd [2000 WL 345159] [17]*

142 *Sienkiewicz v Grief (UK) Ltd [2011] UKSC 10 [90]*

143 *Dr Sido John v Central Manchester and Manchester Children's University Hospitals NHS Foundation Trust [2016] EWHC 407 (QB)*

returning to work owing to the injury sustained in his fall. Regarding future earnings, a reduction was made to the claimant's likely level of attainment at work to reflect the impact of the non-negligent aspects of his injury.

The court found that whilst the effect of the negligent and non-negligent agents on the brain injury was indivisible, damages should nevertheless be reduced giving credit in respect of the injuries that would have been incurred in any event.

Some support for this approach may be drawn from cases of psychiatric injury. The case of *Hatton*[144] was one of four cases that were heard together by the Court of Appeal in respect of stress at work claims. Hale LJ undertook a review of the case law in respect of apportionment and quantification in respect of psychiatric injury. The judge summarised her conclusions in a number of practical propositions[145]. In the case of *Konczak*[146], Underhill LJ identified two of Hale LJ's propositions to be the most relevant when considering apportionment and assessment of damages:

> *(15) Where the harm suffered has more than one cause, the employer should only pay for that proportion of the harm suffered which is attributable to his wrongdoing, unless the harm is truly indivisible. It is for the defendant to raise the question of apportionment.*
>
> *(16) The assessment of damages will take account of any pre-existing disorder or vulnerability and of the chance that the claimant would have succumbed to a stress related disorder in any event.*

---

[144] *Hatton v Sunderland [2002] ICR 613*

[145] *Hatton v Sunderland [2002] ICR 613 [43]*

[146] *BAe Systems (Operations) Limited v Konczak [2018] ICR*

The approach *in Hatton* therefore provides some context for a deduction applying 'but for' principles to a pre-existing condition. In the case of *John*, the pre-existing condition was the non-negligent fall.

Principles of apportionment in cases of a divisible injury were considered in the case of *CNZ*[147].This was a birth injury case whereby a delay in delivery led to led profound hypoxic ischemia (PHI) (see *Material contribution in brain injury cases*). Ritchie J sitting at the High Court considered that the broad-brush approach to the apportionment of damages as applied in the cases of *Thompson*[148](occupational deafness) and *Allen*[149](vibration white finger) was not relevant to his determination of damages as in the index case the award in respect of cerebral palsy was very large.

> *"In my judgment these authorities would support a ruling in the present case that a fair way to apportion the damages in a brain damage case caused by acute PHI at birth would be by way of a percentage based on the relative durations of the PHI caused by the breach compared to the PHI which would have been suffered in any event. This is so even though none of the parties and none of the medical experts supported the percentage apportionment approach in this case until closing when defence counsel, in answer to a question from the Court, did support percentage apportionment based on relative PHI duration. I consider apportionment in law to be a judicial decision arising from the evidence not the medical decision of an expert. But is the evidence sufficient to permit apportionment?"*[150]

147 *CNZ (Suing By Her Father and Litigation Friend MNZ) v Royal Bath Hospitals NHS Foundation Trust and Another [2023] EWHC 19 (KB)*

148 *Thompson v Smiths [1984] QB 405*

149 *Allen v British Railways [2001] ICR 942*

150 *CNZ (Suing By Her Father and Litigation Friend MNZ) v Royal Bath Hospitals NHS Foundation Trust and Another [2023] EWHC 19 (KB) [374]*

In answering his question, Ritchie J considered the findings in *Bailey, Popple and Williams*[151]. The common theme in these cases was, in the judge's opinion, the existence of a gap in the scientific knowledge preventing apportionment. Ritchie J compared the case of *CNZ* to that of *John* in which having considered the expert evidence it was found that apportioning loss was impossible as compared with merely difficult:

> *"I accept that there is a distinction to be drawn between impossibility of proof for apportionment of functional outcome and difficulty over proof for apportionment of functional outcome. The dividing line depends on the evidence. I consider that in the case before me, where the Claimant's cerebral palsy has been caused by one noxious factor: acute PHI, and where the agreed medical evidence is that every minute of PHI caused increasing brain damage, the scientific gap is how to attribute the breach PHI (or each minute of brain damage) to each or any functional deficit"*[152]

<u>Chapter Summary</u>

i. In cases of multiple tortfeasors, the basis assumption is that each one will only be liable for the damage that they have caused.

ii. Apportioning the damage in cases of multiple tortfeasors will be most easily accomplished where there is one causative agent that has operated consecutively in the context of a divisible injury or disease.

iii. Where the outcome of the injury or disease is indivisible or the causative agents have acted concurrently, apportionment is less likely to be possible. Where the apportionment is impossible (as

---

[151] Williams v The Bermuda Hospitals Board [2016] UKPC

[152] *CNZ (Suing By Her Father and Litigation Friend MNZ) v Royal Bath Hospitals NHS Foundation Trust and Another [2023] EWHC 19 (KB) [383]*

opposed to merely difficult) on account of a gap in scientific understanding, the claimant may recover on 100% basis.

CHAPTER NINE

CONSECUTIVE AND CONCURRENT CAUSATIVE AGENTS

In *Bonnington Castings* the negligent and non-negligent causative agents operated concurrently. In other cases, the causative agents have been demonstrated to operate consecutively. The cases of *Williams*[153], *John*[154] and *CNZ*[155] are all examples of the latter. The relevance of sequence was considered by Lord Simon in the case of *McGhee*[156] where the effect of the negligent brick dust caused by the failure to provide washing facilities effectively operated at a different time from the non-negligent brick dust:

> "*Bonnington Castings Ltd. v. Wardlaw [1956] A.C. 613 and Nicholson v. Atlas Steel Foundry Engineering Co. Ltd. [1957] 1 W.L.R. 613 establish, in my view, that where an injury is caused by two (or more) factors operating cumulatively, one (or more) of which factors is a breach of duty and one (or more) is not so, in such a way that it is impossible to ascertain the proportion in which the factors were effective in producing the injury or which factor was decisive, the law does not require a pursuer or plaintiff to prove the impossible, but holds that he is entitled to damages for the injury if he proves on a balance of*

---

153 Williams v The Bermuda Hospitals Board [2016] UKPC [32]

154 *Dr Sido John v Central Manchester and Manchester Children's University Hospitals NHS Foundation Trust [2016] EWHC 407 (QB)*

155 *CNZ (Suing By Her Father and Litigation Friend MNZ) v Royal Bath Hospitals NHS Foundation Trust and Another [2023] EWHC 19 (KB)*

156 *McGhee v National Coal Board 1973 S.C. (H.L.) [37]*

> *probabilities that the breach or breaches of duty contributed substantially to causing the injury. If such factors operate cumulatively, it is, in my judgment, immaterial whether they do so concurrently or successively."*

This point was expanded on by Lord Bridge in his judgment in *Wilsher*:

> *"A distinction is, of course, apparent between the facts of Bonnington Castings Ltd. v. Wardlaw, where the "innocent" and "guilty" silica dust particles which together caused the pursuer's lung disease were inhaled concurrently and the facts of McGhee v. National Coal Board [1973] 1 W.L.R. 1 where the "innocent" and "guilty" brick dust was present on the pursuer's body for consecutive periods.*
>
> *In the one case the concurrent inhalation of "innocent" and "guilty" dust must both have contributed to the cause of the disease. In the other case the consecutive periods when "innocent" and "guilty" brick dust was present on the pursuer's body may both have contributed to the cause of the disease or, theoretically at least, one or other may have been the sole cause.*
>
> *But where the layman is told by the doctors that the longer the brick dust remains on the body, the greater the risk of dermatitis, although the doctors cannot identify the process of causation scientifically, there seems to be nothing irrational in drawing the inference, as a matter of common sense, that the consecutive periods when brick dust remained on the body probably contributed cumulatively to the causation of the dermatitis. I believe that a process of inferential reasoning on these general lines underlies the decision of the majority in McGhee's case"*[157].

Lord Toulson in *Williams* observed that the sequence of events may be relevant where a later event has made a material contribution to the

---

[157] *Wilsher v Essex Area Health Authority [1988] 2 W.L.R. 557* [1087]

outcome as illustrated by the case of *Hotson*[158]. *In Hotson*, the bleeding epiphyseal blood vessels potentially caused negligent damage after the initial non-negligent damage caused at the time of original injury. Lord Toulson contrasted this with a hypothetical situation where an earlier negligent event is overtaken by later events so that the earlier event no longer made a material contribution to the outcome. The Privy Council concluded that "*As a matter of principle, successive events are capable of each making a material contribution to the subsequent outcome*"[159].

In *John*, the claimant suffered a sequence of damaging events that the judge considered materially contributed to his brain injury. The expert evidence was that the function of the brain was sophisticated to the extent that the anatomical areas of damage did not necessarily correlate to the claimant's functional loss "*Dr Ford explained that slow processing speed (a global function) will adversely affect word finding (primarily a left hemisphere function) and working memory and processing speed (both global functions) underpin executive function (primarily a frontal lobe function)*"[160]. On that basis the expert in John considered that the effect of later injury caused by the non-negligent post-operative infection would not have overtaken the earlier negligence but rather have added to the damage that was already there.

---

158 *Hotson v East Berkshire Health Authority [1987] AC 750*

159 Williams v The Bermuda Hospitals Board [2016] UKPC [39]

160 *Dr Sido John v Central Manchester and Manchester Children's University Hospitals NHS Foundation Trust [2016] EWHC 407 (QB) [104]*

CHAPTER TEN

LIMITATIONS ON THE APPLICATION OF MATERIAL CONTRIBUTION

Two cases both heard in 2021, considered that material contribution would have not been applicable to their facts because the injuries were indivisible. The judges in *Thorley* and *Davies* considered themselves bound on the issue of material contribution by the judgments of the Court of Appeal in *AB*[161] and *Heneghan*[162].

In *AB*, Smith LJ when considering the notional prospects of the claimants (the Atomic Veterans) stated that cancer was not a divisible disease to which material contribution could apply. She contrasted the claimants' circumstances in *AB* to the case of *Bailey* which she described as a divisible injury to which material contribution rightfully applied.

It is noteworthy that in Smith LJ's judgment in *Dickens*[163] (see *Material Contribution in Psychiatric Injury Cases*) she referred to the injury in *Bailey* as indivisible. One of the issues considered by Smith LJ in *Dickens* was the apportionment of damages in the context of a psychiatric injury that had been materially contributed to by the defendant. Smith LJ's judgment in *Dickens* did not state or imply that material contribution can only apply to divisible injuries. Rather, that indivisible injuries cannot easily be apportioned.

---

161 *AB v Ministry of Defence [2010] EWCA Civ. 1317*

162 *Heneghan v Manchester Dry Docks Ltd & Others [2016] EWCA Civ 86*

163 *Dickens v O2 Plc [2008] EWCA Civ 1144*

In *Heneghan,* Lord Dyson giving the lead judgment of the Court of Appeal set out three discrete ways of establishing causation in a disease case[164]:

i. Showing that but for the defendant's negligence, the claimant would not have suffered the disease.

ii. Where the disease is caused by the cumulative effect of an agency part of which is attributable to breach of duty on the part of the defendant and part of which involves no breach of duty, the defendant will be liable on the ground that his breach of duty made a 'material contribution' to the disease as per *Bonnington Castings* in which the pneumoconiosis was a divisible disease.

iii. Where causation cannot be proved in either of these ways, for example because the disease is indivisible, causation may be established if it is proved that the defendant materially increased the risk of the victim contracting the disease: the Fairchild exception. Mesothelioma is an indivisible disease.

<u>Davies v Frimley Health NHS Foundation Trust [2021] EWHC 169</u>

The claim was brought by the widower and executor following the death of his wife from pneumococcal meningitis. The deceased had complained of a headache and had been diagnosed with an ear infection by her GP who commenced her on oral antibiotics. The following day she was conveyed by ambulance to the defendant's hospital where she arrived around 09.10. CT scan revealed the presence of intracranial air (pneumocephalus). Antibiotics were administered at 13.20. By 14.30 her level of consciousness began to decrease. She was transferred to intensive care and died the following day.

---

164 *Heneghan v Manchester Dry Docks Ltd & Others [2016] EWCA Civ 86 [23]*

The matter was heard before HHJ Auerbach sitting as a High Court Judge. Prior to the trial, the defendant had admitted that there was a failure to administer antibiotics by 10.40. The only matter for HHJ Auerbach was that of causation that was pleaded applying "but for" causation or in the alternative material contribution. The defendant expressly contended that material contribution was not applicable.

The expert evidence was that the pneumococcal bacteria had likely originated from the ear infection before penetrating the meninges (lining of the brain) either via direct transmission through the bone or indirectly through the blood steam. Thereafter the bacteria and the associated inflammatory response likely caused swelling, raised intracranial pressure and brain ischemia. It was agreed that appropriate treatment would have been by the timely administration of antibiotics at some point prior to the development of ischemia. In order to treat the infection in the meninges, the antibiotics would have to cross the blood-brain barrier. There was disagreement between the experts as to whether the administration of appropriate antibiotics at 10.40 would have altered the outcome. The neurosurgical experts agreed that there was likely "*a time before which the balance of probability favoured survival, a later time after which the balance pointed to death, and a period of uncertainty in between*"[165].

The Judge undertook a detailed analysis of expert evidence based on the deceased's clinical presentation before and after the alleged breach of duty. He concluded that by 10.40, the deceased had not reached the tipping point whereby the administration of antibiotics would have failed to alter the outcome. He therefore found for the claimant applying 'but for' causation.

HHJ Auerbach went on to consider the claimant's alternative case that the failure to administer antibiotics materially contributed to her death. The judge distinguished material contribution as set out in *Bonnington*

[165] *Davies v Frimley Health NHS Foundation Trust [2021] EWHC 169 [94]*

and *Bailey*, from material increase in risk as set out in *Fairchild*. A more critical distinction was drawn between circumstances where material contribution could be applied based on the divisibility of the injury. The judge referred to the description by Lord Phillips in *Sienkiewicz* regarding the characteristics of diseases in terms of their divisibility[166].

HHJ Auerbach cited the following passage from *AB*:

> *"[referring to Bonnington Castings] This type of modification of the 'but for' rule is still available where the negligent and non-negligent causative components have both contributed to the disease (as opposed to the risk of the disease) and it is not possible to apportion the harm caused and therefore the damages. This method of proving causation (by showing that the tort made a material contribution to the condition or disease) is only available where the severity of the disease is related to the amount of exposure; further exposure to the noxious substance in question is capable of making the condition worse"*[167]

In cases with multiple causative agents, HHJ Auerbach framed the issues in terms of apportionment. He summarised the types of cases in which he considered that apportioning of damages could occur as follows[168]:

i. Where the harm is divisible, a party will be liable if their culpable conduct made a contribution to the harm, to the extent of that contribution.

ii. Where the harm is indivisible, a party will be liable for the whole of it, if they caused it, applying "but for" principles.

---

166 *Sienkiewicz v Grief (UK) Ltd [2011] UKSC 10 [12-15]*

167 *AB v Ministry of Defence [2010] EWCA Civ. 1317 [134]*

168 *Davies v Frimley Health NHS Foundation Trust [2021] EWHC 169 [200]*

iii. Thirdly, if two wrongdoers have both caused an indivisible injury, in respect of which it is impossible to apportion liability between them, then each is co-liable for the whole of the injury suffered. HHJ Auerbach considered "*that this approach may, at least in some sub-permutations, be seen as a modification of the 'but for' test, but it is doctrinally well-established and accepted: Konczak points to the fuller discussion in Rahman v Arearose Limited [2001] QB351*".

In terms of the applicability of material contribution, HHJ Auerbach stated:

> "*It seems to me that what the authorities since Bonnington Castings have wrestled with, is whether that decision establishes the existence, outside of Fairchild cases, of an additional route to liability, for either the whole or part of the harm suffered, that may be available where none of the routes I have referred to at [200] above applies, and which is conceptually distinct from all of them. One of the hazards when seeking to interpret the discussion in the later authorities, is that labels like "material contribution" and "cumulative cause case" are not always used in the same sense. Their use does not necessarily signify that the Court is contemplating that some such additional route to liability may be, or does, apply. Sometimes they are used merely to signify that a case is, or maybe, of the first or third orthodox types, or, potentially, one or the other. Sometimes what is meant is less than clear*"[169].

The judge considered that the Court of Appeal in *Bailey* had applied *Bonnington Castings* as a novel means of establishing causation where in the absence of an appropriate means of apportioning the damage, the claimant was awarded damages on a 100% basis. He interpreted *AB* as

[169] *Davies v Frimley Health NHS Foundation Trust [2021] EWHC 169 [202]*

authority for the principle that apportionment of harm should be the focus of the exercise rather than the consideration of material contribution in establishing causation.

HHJ Auerbach pointed to the analysis of *Bonnington Castings* as set out in *AB,* H*eneghan* and *Sinkiewicz* that considered the pneumoconiosis to have been a divisible injury that had not been apportioned. He implied that Smith LJ's use of the term "*material contribution*" in *AB* to have been inaccurate:

> "*The Court in AB was using 'material contribution', I think, to simply refer to a divisible harm type of case*"[170]

HHJ Auerbach concluded that the concept of material contribution was not a novel legal principle but rather one that is has only been applicable to "*a tightly circumscribed type of case*"[171]. On his analysis of the authorities, the principal focus of the jurisprudence since Bonnington was one of divisibility in relation to apportionment, rather than the applicability of material contribution.

<u>Thorley v Sandwell and West Birmingham NHS Trust [2021] EWHC 2604</u>

Thorley was a clinical negligence case heard before Soole J sitting in the High Court. The Claimant was known to have atrial fibrillation (AF). This is an irregularity of the heartbeat that carries a known risk of the development of a blood clot (thrombus) within the heart. These clots tend to then travel (embolize) in the blood vessels to the brain where they can lodge causing a thromboembolic stroke. The claimant was treated prophylactically with warfarin, an anticoagulant, to reduce the risk of clot formation within the heart. It was noted by the judge that the warfarin does not dissolve thrombi which had already formed, nor therefore affect

---

[170] *Davies v Frimley Health NHS Foundation Trust [2021] EWHC 169 [203]*

[171] Ibid [209]

the consequent risk of thromboembolism[172]. The effect of warfarin on the coagulation of the blood is measured with reference to the INR. The standard therapeutic range for warfarin is an INR between 2-3.

The claimant was scheduled to have a cardiac angiogram procedure at the defendant hospital as part of an investigation into chest pain. The claimant was advised to stop taking warfarin prior to the procedure to reduce the risk of bleeding from the cardiac catheter. The claimant was instructed to cease warfarin for four days before the procedure and restart it two days after the procedure at a lower dose. In total, he did not take warfarin for six days. At the time of the angiogram, the claimant's INR was 1.3. The day after restarting his warfarin, the claimant suffered a major stroke. The claimant was left with permanent cognitive and physical disability.

The claimant's amended case was that the warfarin should have been instructed to stop the warfarin three days before the procedure and restart it on the evening of the procedure at his regular dose. The evidence on breach focused on a document that was disclosed late. The defendant accepted that the warfarin should have been recommenced one day earlier and at his regular dose. This admission tallied with the judge's findings. The defendant argued that the claimant would have suffered the stroke in any event.

The claimant's case in causation was pleaded on a 'but for' basis and in the alternative in material contribution. It was not submitted that the case fell within the narrow *'Fairchild exception'*. The judge considered the claimant's alternative cases in causation:

i. 'But for' causation. The claimant's expert accepted that the relationship between INR and stroke risk was more predictable with stable anticoagulation therapy. The expert relied on epidemiological data to demonstrate that with a reduced INR

172 Ibid [8]

there was a reduced relative incidence of strokes. The relative incidence of stroke was less than 50%.

The defendant's hematology expert relied on separate data that suggested that the non-negligent process of weaning off and recommencing warfarin meant the relationship between warfarin dose and INR was unpredictable and exposed the claimant to a higher risk of thromboembolism that had eventuated. The stroke would have occurred in any event.

The court rejected the claimant's case applying "but for" causation. He found that absent the negligent omission of warfarin, the claimant would have suffered stroke in any event.

ii. Material contribution. The evidence of the claimant's hematology expert was that the delay in restarting the warfarin "*made a more than negligible contribution to the occurrence of stroke on a balance of probability*"[173]. Furthermore, the claimant's expert characterised the effect of the breach as materially contributing to the risk of a stroke. The claimant sought to characterise the circumstances as a single causative agent (the absence of warfarin) operating over negligent and non-negligent periods, each of which made a material contribution to the stroke. The period of negligent omission of warfarin thereby materially contributed to the injury.

Soole J analysed the material contribution caselaw. His starting point was that the stroke sustained by the claimant was an indivisible injury "*i.e. which either happens or does not and whose size or severity is unaffected by the dose of warfarin*"[174]. The claimant relied upon the findings of the Privy Council in *Williams* and referred to *Bonnington Castings* and *Bailey* to

[173] Thorley v Sandwell and West Birmingham NHS Trust [2021] EWHC 2604 [86]

[174] Ibid [139]

support the contention that the indivisible nature of the injury was no bar to the application of material contribution, "*the divisibility or indivisibility of injury was relevant only to the measure of damages against the contributing tortfeasor, not to the principle of the application of this modified test of causation*"[175].

The judge however felt bound by the decisions in *AB*, and *Heneghan* where the judgments of the Court of Appeal expressly conveyed that material contribution was inapplicable to cases of an indivisible injury. Soole J also referred to the first instance decision of *Davies*. Soole J found that "*the test of material contribution has no application to a case where (as here) there is indivisible injury and one tortfeasor*"[176]. He considered that the case of *John* was not relevant to his determination.

The judge concluded "*This is evidently a legal issue which is ripe for authoritative review, at least in a case where it may affect the result. On the basis of strict precedent, I conclude that the reasoning of the Court of Appeal in AB and Heneghan must be followed. Accordingly, the claim of material contribution must fail on the basis that this modified test of causation does not apply when there is a single tortfeasor and an indivisible injury*"[177].

<u>Chapter Summary</u>

i. Both cases plead the claimant's case applying 'but for' contribution and material contribution in the alternative. The judges considered the claimant's case in material contribution and strictly applied *AB* and *Heneghan;* material contribution could only be applied to divisible injuries.

---

175 Ibid [141]

176 Ibid [147]

177 Thorley v Sandwell and West Birmingham NHS Trust [2021] EWHC 2604 [151]

ii. In Davies, the judgment of HHJ Auerbach questioned the application of material contribution. HHJ Auerbach characterised the issues faced by the court in cases of multiple tortfeasors as one of apportionment. He characterised *Bonnington Castings* as case that should have been apportioned but was not and proposed alternative interpretations of the findings in cases where material contribution was considered.

iii. The judgment in *Thorley* is informed by the interpretation of material contribution in *Davies*. The conclusion was that material contribution causation does not apply when there is a single tortfeasor and an indivisible injury. *Bailey*[178] and *Williams* are both cases where there was a single tortfeasor and arguably an indivisible outcome. The true interpretation may depend upon whether the term indivisible is referring to the process or in the injury (see *Divisibility and Indivisibility As Sources of Confusion*). Arguably if there is only one suspect, then the 'but for' test would be the appropriate test to apply.

[178] *Bailey v Ministry of Defence [2008] EWCA Civ 883.*

CHAPTER ELEVEN

MATERIAL CONTRIBUTION IN BIRTH INJURY CASES

In birth injury cases breaches commonly involve a delay in identifying signs of fetal distress and a consequent failing to perform earlier delivery. The losses in these cases flow from still births, deaths of the newborn, and other serious non-fatal complications such as cerebral palsy. As with cases such as *Williams*[179], delays may be characterized as comprising negligent and non-negligent periods of time. Injuries sustained have been considered and classified in terms of indivisibility.

> In light of the findings in *Davies*[180] and *Thorley*[181], the claimant in the case of *CNZ*[182] argued that the brain damage caused at birth was a dose related divisible injury to which material contribution could be applied (see *Material Contribution In Brain Injury Cases*)

<u>Popple v Birmingham Women's NHS Foundation Trust [2012] EWCA Civ 1628</u>

> This case was brought by a claimant, who suffered with cerebral palsy. It was alleged that his condition was caused by the management of his labour at the defendant's hospital. The matter was heard at first instance before HHJ Jones QC who

---

179 Williams v The Bermuda Hospitals Board [2016] UKPC

180 *Davies v Frimley Health NHS Foundation Trust [2021] EWHC 169*

181 Thorley v Sandwell and West Birmingham NHS Trust [2021] EWHC 2604

182 CNZ (Suing By Her Father and Litigation Friend MNZ) v Royal Bath Hospitals NHS Foundation Trust and Another [2023] EWHC 19 (KB)

found for the claimant based on negligent delays in the minutes before birth. The matter was appealed on the facts.

The claimant alleged that a pathological fetal heart rate pattern on the CTG was apparent at 14.27, 22 minutes before the claimant was delivered. It was the claimant's case that the in the absence of negligence, expedited delivery (by instrumental delivery and/or episiotomy) should have taken place and the birth would have occurred no later than 14.44.

The experts on both sides accepted that the injury that caused the cerebral palsy was caused by a period of asphyxia for a period of 15-20 minutes. The first 10 minutes of this asphyxia would not likely have caused harm due to fetal reserves. The court was asked to determine when the period of asphyxia likely took place, whether it coincided with the allegations of negligence, or in the alternative whether it happened at an earlier time whereby the damage would have occurred in any event. The judge at first instance found that:

"*even when fetal reserves are exhausted, the sustaining of brain damage was described as a 'process' rather than as a single event...He (counsel for the claimant) went on to submit that medical science is only able to provide a bracket working backwards from the known time of birth and that, on any view, Nathan would have been saved form 5 minutes of damaging hypoxia had he been delivered by 14.44 at the latest*"[183].

Ward LJ gave the judgment on appeal. The causation issued focused upon how much damage would have occurred by 14.44, 5 minutes earlier than when the claimant was born. Some damage might have occurred by 14.44 but the claimant would have avoided 5 minutes of asphyxia. It was impossible to say how

183 Popple v Birmingham Women's NHS Foundation Trust [2012] EWCA Civ 1628 [74]

much, if any, damage had occurred prior to 14.44. It was certain that the period after 14.44 was damaging. On that basis the court concluded that the damage caused by the delay after 14.44 was either causative on a 'but for' basis or in the context of material contribution:

"*Here the negligent failure to deliver Nathan before 14.44 caused all of the damage if this was a 15-minute insult. Medical science cannot establish whether it was a 15-minute insult or a 20-minute insult. If it did take 20 minutes, the damage done in the last five minutes must have made a material contribution to the overall harm which ws more than minimal. I cannot see why the Bailey principle does not apply*"[184]

The Court of Appeal did not consider whether the brain injury was a divisible or indivisible injury nor the potential issue of apportionment.

[184] Popple v Birmingham Women's NHS Foundation Trust [2012] EWCA Civ 1628 [79]

CHAPTER TWELVE

MATERIAL CONTRIBUTION IN BRAIN INJURY CASES

Brain injuries can occur through various means including raised increased pressure within the vault of the skull caused by trauma or infection, or a reduction in blood supply. The final mechanism in most cases is the interruption of the supply of oxygen to brain tissues thereby causing ischemia.

The issue that made apportionment impossible in *John*[185] was the inability of the medical experts to attribute the separate injuries sustained in the fall, the period of raised intracranial pressure, and the postoperative infection. The other issue was the correlation between the injury and its effect upon the claimant's level of function. A similar issue was identified in *CNZ.*

The case of *Davies* considered the circumstances of death by bacterial meningitis. The judge found for the claimant applying 'but for' causation. The evidence of one of the expert neurosurgeons was that one period of the delay in giving antibiotics materially contributed to the claimant's death. Other evidence suggested that the delay only increased the risk of death. The meningitis was a potentially divisible cumulative process, akin perhaps to the sepsis in *Williams*, or the weakness in *Bailey*. HHJ Auerbach did not consider it to be a case of to which material contribution could be applied.

---

185 *Dr Sido John v Central Manchester and Manchester Children's University Hospitals NHS Foundation Trust [2016] EWHC 407 (QB)*

Ayesha Canning-Kishver (By Her Mother and Litigation Friend Shahana Kishver) v Sandwell & West Birmingham Hospitals NHS Trust [2008] EWHC 2384 (QB)

The case involved allegations of negligent treatment of the claimant causative of brain damage. The claimant was born prematurely at the defendant's hospital. It was the claimant's case that there had been a delay in the assessment and treatment of her deterioration whilst being cared for at the neonatal unit which had caused or materially contributed to cerebellar atrophy and her consequent disabilities.

The expert evidence was that the cause of cerebellar atrophy was at the time subject to research and thereby was speculative "*the current issues were at the 'cutting edge'!*"[186]. The defendant argued that was insufficient evidence to establish a causal connection.

Sir Christopher Holland, having found breach of duty, was unable to find for causation applying 'but for' principles. In his summary on causation the judge accepted that there were other possible causes for the claimant's injury but considered "*there is nothing that suggests that that non tortious cause was probable*"[187]. He considered the judgment of Waller LJ in *Bailey* to be of assistance in determining causation, concluding that on balance of probabilities the contribution occasioned by the breach of duty constituted a contribution to the atrophy of the cerebellum that was more than negligible.

[186] Ayesha Canning-Kishver (By Her Mother and Litigation Friend Shahana Kishver) v Sandwell & West Birmingham Hospitals NHS Trust [2008] EWHC 2384 (QB) [30]

[187] Ayesha Canning-Kishver (By Her Mother and Litigation Friend Shahana Kishver) v Sandwell & West Birmingham Hospitals NHS Trust [2008] EWHC 2384 (QB) [37]

CNZ (Suing By Her Father and Litigation Friend MNZ) v Royal Bath Hospitals NHS Foundation Trust and Another [2023] EWHC 19 (KB)

The claimant in this case was a 26-year woman with cerebral palsy born at 01.03 on 3 February 1996. The claimant was born following the birth of her twin approximately one hour before. The claimant alleged that her condition was a result of acute profound hypoxic ischemia (PHI) sustained in the minutes before and after she was born. It was the claimant's case that her mother requested or should have been offered a caesarian section and that had one been performed in a timely manner the claimant would have avoided her injury. In addition, it was alleged that the defendant failed to acknowledge or respond to concerning features of the CTG and should have acted more swiftly following the birth of her twin.

The claimant's pleaded case on causation was that the injury was likely all or nothing "*every minute counts and that even a short delay would have made a material contribution which should lead to a 100% recovery because the functional result of a few minutes of negligently caused acute PHI is indivisible from the total injury suffered*"[188]. The defendant accepted that had she been born before 00.55 she would have avoided her injury altogether. Between 00.55 and 01.03, her injury would have been less. The defendant contended that during those eight minutes, the claimant's injury was potentially divisible. Less time starved of oxygen equated to less PHI and less brain damage.

Richie J sitting in the High Court found the treating clinician's inexperience had led to a delay in delivery. Absent the negligence, the claimant would have been born between 00.55 and 00.58, giving a total negligent delay of between five and eight minutes (midpoint of 6.5

---

188 CNZ (Suing By Her Father and Litigation Friend MNZ) v Royal Bath Hospitals NHS Foundation Trust and Another [2023] EWHC 19 (KB) [38]

minutes). In the case of this earlier delivery, the period of resuscitation would also have been reduced.

In relation to medical causation, the judge heard evidence that the first 10 minutes of oxygen asphyxiation would not likely have caused any harm due to fetal reserves and ability of the fetus to compensate. The claimant's pediatric neurology expert described the relationship between PHI and functionality as *"certainly not linear"* because different populations of brain cells were described as having different vulnerabilities to low oxygen "*they would cope and then they would 'fall of the cliff'*"[189]. It was therefore difficult to extrapolate the period of PHI from the claimant's level of disability. The judge adopted the claimant's expert's estimated range of PHI to be between 14 and 18 minutes (midpoint 16 minutes).

Overall, the judge considered that the delay was causative of the whole of the claimant's brain damage. Given that brain damage would not have occurred in the first 10 minutes of PHI, saving 6.5 minutes would on the balance of probabilities have avoided it all[190]

Having found for claimant applying standard causation principles, the judge went on to consider the claimant's case had he found the claimant's injury to have been caused by periods of negligent and non-negligent PHI. As a starting point he affirmed that the burden of proof would have been on the claimant to demonstrate that the "*breaches caused injury distinct from and beyond the injury caused by the PHI which was non negligent*"[191].

The agreed evidence of the pediatric neonatologists was that every minute of asphyxia beyond the first 10 minutes caused incremental brain damage. The judge concluded that this damage would have been more

---

[189] Ibid [236].

[190] Ibid [323].

[191] Ibid [325]

than *de minimis*. Furthermore, the damage caused would have increased the claimant's functional disability. Applying 'but for' causation, the claimant would still have discharged her burden of proving injury. The judge considered however that the quantification of functional loss was impossible. The experts "*could not predict the pattern or severity of the resulting functional disability from a minute-by-minute increase in the duration of the PHI suffered*"[192].

On the alternative basis that every minute of PHI had made a material contribution to the brain damage, the court went on to consider whether this should nevertheless be reflected in an apportionment of quantum. The judge undertook a review of the caselaw and identified a number of relevant characteristics of material contribution that applied to the index case:

i. Two tests for causation may be applied in a case of brain injury caused by asphyxia. The first was the "but for" test, followed by the material contribution test in relation to the functional outcome of the injury[193].

ii. The test of material contribution to injury can apply where the 'but for' test cannot be satisfied due to the existence of an impossible gap in proving something scientifically[194].

iii. The concept of material contribution of risk (as per *Fairchild*) of causing the injury had more limited application and was not relevant to the index case[195].

---

[192] Ibid [327].

[193] Ibid [326]

[194] Ibid [341]

[195] Ibid [350]

iv. The case involved only one potential causative agent (the PHI) and could thereby be distinguished from the facts from *Wilsher*[196].

v. Applying the notions of divisibility and indivisibility (Lord Phillips in *Sienkiewicz*), the index claimant's injury was more easily characterised as a divisible or dose related injury (as opposed to a trigger case):

> "*I do not consider that the term indivisible applies to the Claimant's brain injuries in this case. An indivisible disease is one which starts when triggered and then goes on and gets worse or takes its course whatever the exposure to the noxious substance after the triggering event. These diseases are not divisible in the sense that they are not reduced by stopping the exposure and do not get worse on increasing the exposure. They start and then they progress, like cancer or mesothelioma.*
>
> *Brain damage caused by PHI is not a trigger disease. It does not grow like cancer or mesothelioma once triggered. The spread of brain damage due to PHI is wholly dose dependent. The more PHI the fetus suffers the greater the brain damage. However, the word indivisible may apply to the functional outcome caused by one or more minutes of acute PHI*"[197]

vi. Where the injury caused by asphyxia is divisible, it may be appropriate to apportion damages based on the relative

[196] Ibid [355]

[197] Ibid [361]

durations caused by the period of breach compared to the period of asphyxia that was non-negligent[198].

vii. There is a distinction between cases where the apportioning of functional outcome is difficult as opposed to apportioning being impossible. Ritchie J did not accept the expert neurological evidence that an extent of the functional damage could be measured with reference to the period of asphyxia divided up into "*aliquots*" of 5 minutes[199].

Richie J identified *Williams and Bailey* as cases where the available evidence made apportionment impossible. He considered that the index case was similar, and had the need to apply material contribution arose, then due to the gap in scientific understanding in correlating the period of asphyxiation with the functional outcome, the claimant would have received damages on a 100% basis. Apportionment based on the relative periods of negligent and non-negligent asphyxia would have only been appropriate had the medical evidence allowed. Under the circumstances he considered that apportionment would have been impossible.

198 Ibid [374]

199 Ibid [383]

CHAPTER THIRTEEN

MATERIAL CONTRIBUTION IN PSYCHIATRIC INJURY CASES

Psychiatric damage is a not uncommon feature of clinical negligence cases. A claimant who has suffered loss on account of alleged clinical negligence may bring a claim for damages as a primary psychiatric victim. Such an injury may be alleged, for example, by a mother following a negligent stillbirth. The position of the law on secondary victims in clinical negligence cases is at the time of writing awaiting the judgment of the Supreme Court in the case of *Paul*[200].

The focus of this section is not material contribution in respect of primary physical injury but rather in the context of claims arising in respect of psychiatric damage where there are potentially competing causative agents. In that context, the courts have applied concepts of divisibility and apportionment and have considered the same case law that deals with material contribution in general. It is for those reasons that it is deserving of some attention.

A tortious psychiatric injury can occur in the context of other non-negligent causative agents that may be found to have contributed to the overall psychiatric presentation. In these types of cases, it may not be possible for a claimant to prove applying 'but for' causation principles that absent the negligence, the claimant would have avoided the injury. A claimant may therefore plead their case in material contribution on the basis that the effect of the negligent causative agent was more than

[200] Paul and another (Appellants) v Royal Wolverhampton NHS Trust (Respondent) [2022] EWCA Civ 12

minimal. It may be appropriate to apportion the losses between the various causes.

In *Hatton*[201], the Court of Appeal considered the circumstances of a claim for stress at work. In that case Hale LJ stated the following in relation to causation:

> "*It is still necessary to show that the particular breach of duty found caused the harm. It is not enough to show that occupational stress caused the harm. Where there are several different possible causes, as will often be the case with stress related illness of any kind, the claimant may have difficulty in proving that the employer's fault was one of them: see Wilsher v Essex Area Health Authority [1988] AC 1074. This will be a particular problem if…the main cause was a vulnerable personality which the employer knew nothing about. However, the employee does not have to show that the breach of duty was the whole cause of his ill-health: it is enough to show that it made a material contribution.* : see *Bonnington Castings v Wardlaw [1956] AC 613*"[202].

In obiter Hale LJ giving judgment in *Hatton* endorsed apportionment in the case of psychiatric injury to which a tortfeasor has materially contributed. This generally applied to cases both where the injury was divisible and where it was indivisible. The apportionment of damages reflected the claimant's likely future vulnerability to a psychiatric injury.

The case of *Rahman*[203] remains a leading case in the apportionment of damages in the context of psychiatric loss. In that case the claimant sustained both physical and associated psychiatric damage whilst

---

201 *Hatton v Sunderland [2002] ICR 613*

202 Ibid [35].

203 *Rahman v Arearose Limited & University College London NHS Trust 2000 WL 741943*

assaulted in the course of his employment. The claimant went on to receive substandard medical treatment that caused him to become blind in one eye. In R*ahman* Laws LJ considered the psychiatric injury was made up of distinct components that were capable of being apportioned between the employer and the treating hospital.

<u>Dickens v O2 Plc [2008] EWCA Civ 1144</u>

The case of *Dickens* was a stress-at-work claim brought by a regulatory finance manager against her employer. The claimant's job involved auditing, which she found extremely stressful. She alleged that the defendant had failed to heed her warnings that her mental health was deteriorating and assist in relieving her situation. HHJ Corrie at first instance found for the claimant with reference to the guidance set out in the case of Court of Appeal case of *Hatton (*and endorsed by the House of Lords in *Barber*[204]*).* Damages were apportioned and the judge reducing the claimed damages by 50% to reflect non-tortious factors.

The defendant appealed on the basis that *inter alia* the judge had erred in his approach to causation "*He had held only that the appellant's breach had increased the risk of the respondent suffering injury to health; he had not found that it had made a material contribution to the injury*"[205]. The lead judgement of the Court of Appeal was delivered by Smith LJ.

In relation to causation of psychiatric harm, the defendant referred to the judgment of the Court of Appeal in *Hatton*. Smith LJ considered whether it had been appropriate to apportion the damages on account of negligent and non-negligent causative factors. The judge referred to *Bailey*[206] in which negligent and non-negligent causative agents had contributed to the claimant's weakness. Having found for the claimant in *Bailey* on the

204 *Barber v Somerset County Council [2004] ICR 457*

205 *Dickens v O2 Plc [2008] EWCA Civ 1144* [4].

206 *Bailey v Ministry of Defence [2008] EWCA Civ 883*

basis of material contribution, no apportionment of the damages was made. Smith LJ (who was one of the panel in *Bailey*) commented:

> "*My immediate reaction to the question of apportionment in the instant appeal was to wonder whether this case was any different from Bailey. Was this not a case of an indivisible injury (the respondent's seriously damaged state following her breakdown) with more than one cause? It was not possible to say that, but for the tort, the respondent would probably not have suffered the breakdown but it was possible to say that the tort had made a material contribution to it. If that is a correct analysis, should not the starting point have been that the respondent was entitled to recover in full?*"[207]

Smith LJ went on to consider whether faced with an "*indivisible injury*" the court could perform an apportionment exercise "*It seems to me that, if in one breath the judge holds that all that can be said about the effect of the tort is that it made an unspecified material contribution, it is illogical for him, in the next breath, to attempt to assess the percentage effect of the tort as a basis for apportionment of the whole of the damages. That is not to say that it is not important to have in mind in assessing damages the condition of the claimant before any tortious act occurred*".[208]

Smith LJ stated that apportionment applies to divisible injuries but not convinced of the appropriateness of such an exercise in a psychiatric injury with multiple causes, raising doubts about the correctness of Hale LJ's approach to apportionment in *Hatton*. Smith LJ concluded:

> "*In a case which has had to be decided on the basis that the tort has made a material contribution but it is not scientifically possible to say how much that contribution is (apart from the assessment that it was more than de minimis) and where the*

207 *Dickens v O2 Plc [2008] EWCA Civ 1144 [42]*

208 Dickens v O2 Plc [2008] EWCA Civ 1144 [43]

injury to which that has lead is indivisible, it will be inappropriate simply to apportion the damages across the board. It may well be appropriate to bear in mind that the claimant was psychiatrically vulnerable and might have suffered a breakdown at some time in the future even without the tort. There may then be a reduction in some heads of damage for future risks of non-tortious loss. But my provisional view is that there should not be any rule that the judge should apportion the damages across the board merely because one non-tortious cause has been in play"[209]

Sedley LJ agreed with the findings of Smith LJ:

"I…am troubled by the shared assumption about the appropriateness of apportionment on which the case has proceeded. While the law does not expect tortfeasors to pay for damage that they have not caused, it regards them as having caused damage to which they have materially contributed. Such damage may be limited in its arithmetical purchase where one can quantify the possibility that it would have occurred sooner or later in any event; but that is quite different from apportioning the damage itself between tortious and non-tortious causes. The latter may become admissible where the aetiology of the injury makes it truly divisible, but that is not this case. While the obiter dicta of Hale LJ in Hatton are, as always, entitled to the greatest respect, the stare decisis principle requires courts of first instance, at least for the present, to take their cue in this regard from Bailey… "[210]

209 Dickens v O2 Plc [2008] EWCA Civ 1144 [46]

210 Ibid [53]

BAE Systems (Operations) Limited v Marion Konczak [2017] EWCA Civ 1188

The case of *Konczak* was brought by an employee alleging sex discrimination in the course of her employment and dismissal. The claimant alleged that the defendant had breached their duty to her which had caused or materially contributed to her mental ill health. It was found that the claimant had a background history of stress and problems at work. The case was heard before the Employment Tribunal (over four substantive hearings). The claimant was awarded damages and the defendant appealed.

Lord Justice Underhill gave the lead judgment in the Court of Appeal. In considering the issues of material contribution and divisibility, the court referred to the cases of *Hatton*[211] and *Dickens*[212]. The court quoted extra-judicial comments made by LJ Smith following her judgment in *Dickens*:

> "*Psychiatry does not lend itself to the kind of statistical analysis which orthopaedic surgeons and oncologists can provide. So the judge is likely to be left with evidence that the claimant had a vulnerable personality and that there was more than one factor in play when he had the breakdown. If that is the state of the evidence, it seems to me that the claimant should succeed in full provided that the negligent factor was of more than minimal effect*"[213].

The court dismissed the defendant's appeal. On the divisibility issue, LJ Underhill concluded:

---

[211] *Hatton v Sunderland [2002] ICR 613*

[212] *Dickens v O2 Plc [2008] EWCA Civ 1144*

[213] *Dickens v O2 Plc [2008] EWCA Civ 1144* [66].

"the tribunal should seek to find a rational basis for distinguishing between a part of the illness which is due to the employer's wrong and a part which is due to other causes; but whether that is possible will depend on the facts and the evidence. If there is no such basis, then the injury will indeed be, in Hale LJ's words, "truly indivisible", and principle requires that the claimant is compensated for the whole of the injury — though, importantly, if (as Smith LJ says will be typically the case) the claimant has a vulnerable personality, a discount may be required"[214]

[214] BAE Systems (Operations) Limited v Marion Konczak [2017] EWCA Civ 1188 [72]

CHAPTER FOURTEEN

OVERALL CONCLUSIONS

Material contribution causation is fluid concept that has been applied to a range of circumstances in clinical negligence. The requirement for an alternative test in causation was born out of circumstances in occupational disease cases where it was impossible to prove that a disease had been caused on the balance of probabilities by the operation of a particular causative agent from a negligent source. The impetus for the courts to develop a more pragmatic test for causation in occupational disease cases was policy driven in favor of employees who had contracted diseases in the course of their employment.

Clinical negligence cases to which material contribution has been applied are similar to occupational disease cases in that negligent and non-negligent causative agents are in operation. In clinical contexts, a common causative agent is time: delay being the negligent version of it. A common feature in clinical negligence cases is that the delay occurs over a short period of time (*Bailey, Williams, John, CNZ*). This feature is likely to be due to the difficulties in separating the operation of causative agents over shorter periods of time.

The current issues regarding divisibility and indivisibility originated from *Bonnington Castings*. Was material contribution applied by the court on the basis that the pneumoconiosis was divisible or indivisible? Was *Bonnington Castings* simply a case of a divisible injury that could have been apportioned? The potential confusion around the application of the terms divisibility and indivisibility has crystalised in the recent cases of *Davies* and *Thorley*. Prior to those cases, faced with multiple potential causative agents, the courts applied material contribution causation to disease processes and outcomes that had both divisible and indivisible characteristics. It is anticipated that the Supreme Court will provide some clarity on this issue.

Any analysis of cases with multiple causative agents should include consideration of the following issues:

1. **Burden of proof.** It is for the claimant to prove that on the balance of probabilities the negligent agent caused or contributed to the injury.

2. **The 'but for' test.** In most cases, causation will succeed or fail in the hands of the traditional test for causation. A tortfeasor takes their victim as they find them. If the non-negligent agent was a pre-existing vulnerability, it may not be necessary to involve material contribution.

3. **Material contribution to the injury itself.** As stated above, this needs to be proven on the balance of probabilities. Material contribution to the risk will not be sufficient for a claimant to succeed. It may be possible to apply epidemiological evidence to demonstrate there to have been a doubling of the risk.

4. **Multiple possible causative agents.** Do these agents form part of a cumulative process or are they discrete, each one of which might have caused the injury? In clinical negligence circumstances this is not an uncommon situation (as per Wilsher[215]).

5. **An indivisible injury.** These are the trigger injures as described by Lord Phillips in *Sienkiewicz*[216]. The term has been used to describe both the process of a disease or injury and the outcome. Death is an indivisible outcome but one that may have been materially contributed to by a negligent causative agent. Mesothelioma is an indivisible disease process for which the *Fairchild* exception was created. In the case of a truly

[215] *Wilsher v Essex Area Health Authority [1988] 2 W.L.R. 557*

[216] *Sienkiewicz v Grief (UK) Ltd [2011] UKSC 10*

indivisible disease process, material contribution is unlikely to apply.

6. **A divisible injury.** Where the causes are cumulative and the negligent and non-negligent components are versions of the same agent. Examples of this are weakness, sepsis, asphyxia, and raised intracranial pressure divisible operating over negligent and non-negligent periods of time.

7. **Apportionment**. A defendant should only be found liable in damages to the extent of their responsibility. Apportionment of a divisible injury or disease may be possible where the evidence allows. The inability to apportion the damage may occur in the context of both divisible and indivisible injuries and diseases.

MORE BOOKS BY LAW BRIEF PUBLISHING

A selection of our other titles available now:-

'A Practical Guide to Estate Administration and Crypto Assets' by Richard Marshall
'A Practical Guide to Managing GDPR Data Subject Access Requests – Second Edition' by Patrick O'Kane
'A Practical Guide to Parental Alienation in Private and Public Law Children Cases' by Sam King QC & Frankie Shama
'Contested Heritage – Removing Art from Land and Historic Buildings' by Richard Harwood QC, Catherine Dobson, David Sawtell
'The Limits of Separate Legal Personality: When Those Running a Company Can Be Held Personally Liable for Losses Caused to Third Parties Outside of the Company' by Dr Mike Wilkinson
'A Practical Guide to Transgender Law' by Robin Moira White & Nicola Newbegin
'A Practical Guide to 'Stranded Spouses' in Family Law' by Mani Singh Basi
'A Practical Guide to Residential Freehold Conveyancing' by Lorraine Richardson
'A Practical Guide to Pensions on Divorce for Lawyers' by Bryan Scant
'A Practical Guide to Challenging Sham Marriage Allegations in Immigration Law' by Priya Solanki
'A Practical Guide to Legal Rights in Scotland' by Sarah-Jane Macdonald
'A Practical Guide to New Build Conveyancing' by Paul Sams & Rebecca East
'A Practical Guide to Defending Barristers in Disciplinary Cases' by Marc Beaumont
'A Practical Guide to Inherited Wealth on Divorce' by Hayley Trim
'A Practical Guide to Practice Direction 12J and Domestic Abuse in Private Law Children Proceedings' by Rebecca Cross & Malvika Jaganmohan
'A Practical Guide to Confiscation and Restraint' by Narita Bahra QC, John Carl Townsend, David Winch
'A Practical Guide to the Law of Forests in Scotland' by Philip Buchan
'A Practical Guide to Health and Medical Cases in Immigration Law' by Rebecca Chapman & Miranda Butler

'A Practical Guide to Bad Character Evidence for Criminal Practitioners by Aparna Rao
'A Practical Guide to Extradition Law post-Brexit' by Myles Grandison et al
'A Practical Guide to Hoarding and Mental Health for Housing Lawyers' by Rachel Coyle
'A Practical Guide to Psychiatric Claims in Personal Injury – 2nd Edition' by Liam Ryan
'Stephens on Contractual Indemnities' by Richard Stephens
'A Practical Guide to the EU Succession Regulation' by Richard Frimston
'A Practical Guide to Solicitor and Client Costs – 2nd Edition' by Robin Dunne
'Constructive Dismissal – Practice Pointers and Principles' by Benjimin Burgher
'A Practical Guide to Religion and Belief Discrimination Claims in the Workplace' by Kashif Ali
'A Practical Guide to the Law of Medical Treatment Decisions' by Ben Troke
'Fundamental Dishonesty and QOCS in Personal Injury Proceedings: Law and Practice' by Jake Rowley
'A Practical Guide to the Law in Relation to School Exclusions' by Charlotte Hadfield & Alice de Coverley
'A Practical Guide to Divorce for the Silver Separators' by Karin Walker
'The Right to be Forgotten – The Law and Practical Issues' by Melissa Stock
'A Practical Guide to Planning Law and Rights of Way in National Parks, the Broads and AONBs' by James Maurici QC, James Neill et al
'A Practical Guide to Election Law' by Tom Tabori
'A Practical Guide to the Law in Relation to Surrogacy' by Andrew Powell
'A Practical Guide to Claims Arising from Fatal Accidents – 2nd Edition' by James Patience
'A Practical Guide to the Ownership of Employee Inventions – From Entitlement to Compensation' by James Tumbridge & Ashley Roughton
'A Practical Guide to Asbestos Claims' by Jonathan Owen & Gareth McAloon
'A Practical Guide to Stamp Duty Land Tax in England and Northern Ireland' by Suzanne O'Hara
'A Practical Guide to the Law of Farming Partnerships' by Philip Whitcomb
'Covid-19, Homeworking and the Law – The Essential Guide to Employment and GDPR Issues' by Forbes Solicitors
'Covid-19 and Criminal Law – The Essential Guide' by Ramya Nagesh

'Covid-19 and Family Law in England and Wales – The Essential Guide' by Safda Mahmood
'A Practical Guide to the Law of Unlawful Eviction and Harassment – 2nd Edition' by Stephanie Lovegrove
'Covid-19, Brexit and the Law of Commercial Leases – The Essential Guide' by Mark Shelton
'A Practical Guide to Costs in Personal Injury Claims – 2nd Edition' by Matthew Hoe
'A Practical Guide to the General Data Protection Regulation (GDPR) – 2nd Edition' by Keith Markham
'Ellis on Credit Hire – Sixth Edition' by Aidan Ellis & Tim Kevan
'A Practical Guide to Working with Litigants in Person and McKenzie Friends in Family Cases' by Stuart Barlow
'Protecting Unregistered Brands: A Practical Guide to the Law of Passing Off' by Lorna Brazell
'A Practical Guide to Secondary Liability and Joint Enterprise Post-Jogee' by Joanne Cecil & James Mehigan
'A Practical Guide to the Pre-Action RTA Claims Protocol for Personal Injury Lawyers' by Antonia Ford
'A Practical Guide to Neighbour Disputes and the Law' by Alexander Walsh
'A Practical Guide to Forfeiture of Leases' by Mark Shelton
'A Practical Guide to Coercive Control for Legal Practitioners and Victims' by Rachel Horman
'A Practical Guide to Rights Over Airspace and Subsoil' by Daniel Gatty
'Tackling Disclosure in the Criminal Courts – A Practitioner's Guide' by Narita Bahra QC & Don Ramble
'A Practical Guide to the Law of Driverless Cars – Second Edition' by Alex Glassbrook, Emma Northey & Scarlett Milligan
'A Practical Guide to TOLATA Claims' by Greg Williams
'A Practical Guide to Elderly Law – 2nd Edition' by Justin Patten
'A Practical Guide to Responding to Housing Disrepair and Unfitness Claims' by Iain Wightwick
'A Practical Guide to the Construction and Rectification of Wills and Trust Instruments' by Edward Hewitt
'A Practical Guide to the Law of Bullying and Harassment in the Workplace' by Philip Hyland

'How to Be a Freelance Solicitor: A Practical Guide to the SRA-Regulated Freelance Solicitor Model' by Paul Bennett
'A Practical Guide to Prison Injury Claims' by Malcolm Johnson
'A Practical Guide to the Small Claims Track - 2nd Edition' by Dominic Bright
'A Practical Guide to Advising Clients at the Police Station' by Colin Stephen McKeown-Beaumont
'A Practical Guide to Antisocial Behaviour Injunctions' by Iain Wightwick
'Practical Mediation: A Guide for Mediators, Advocates, Advisers, Lawyers, and Students in Civil, Commercial, Business, Property, Workplace, and Employment Cases' by Jonathan Dingle with John Sephton
'The Mini-Pupillage Workbook' by David Boyle
'A Practical Guide to Crofting Law' by Brian Inkster
'A Practical Guide to Spousal Maintenance' by Liz Cowell
'A Practical Guide to the Law of Domain Names and Cybersquatting' by Andrew Clemson
'A Practical Guide to the Law of Gender Pay Gap Reporting' by Harini Iyengar
'NHS Whistleblowing and the Law' by Joseph England
'Employment Law and the Gig Economy' by Nigel Mackay & Annie Powell
'A Practical Guide to Noise Induced Hearing Loss (NIHL) Claims' by Andrew Mckie, Ian Skeate, Gareth McAloon
'An Introduction to Beauty Negligence Claims – A Practical Guide for the Personal Injury Practitioner' by Greg Almond
'Intercompany Agreements for Transfer Pricing Compliance' by Paul Sutton
'Zen and the Art of Mediation' by Martin Plowman
'A Practical Guide to the SRA Principles, Individual and Law Firm Codes of Conduct 2019 – What Every Law Firm Needs to Know' by Paul Bennett
'A Practical Guide to Adoption for Family Lawyers' by Graham Pegg
'A Practical Guide to Industrial Disease Claims' by Andrew Mckie & Ian Skeate
'A Practical Guide to Redundancy' by Philip Hyland
'A Practical Guide to Vicarious Liability' by Mariel Irvine
'A Practical Guide to Applications for Landlord's Consent and Variation of Leases' by Mark Shelton
'A Practical Guide to Relief from Sanctions Post-Mitchell and Denton' by Peter Causton

www.ingramcontent.com/pod-product-compliance
Lightning Source LLC
LaVergne TN
LVHW022055200926
848481LV00003B/919

* 9 7 8 1 9 1 6 6 9 8 1 3 0 *